STILL SEEKING JUSTICE

STILL SEEKING JUSTICE

Reform and Redress of
Japan's Flawed Judicial System

Compiled by
HIROMASA EZOE

FOUNDER OF RECRUIT

KODANSHA INTERNATIONAL
Tokyo • New York • London

Originally published in Japanese in 2009 by Chuokoronshinsha, Tokyo, under the title *Torishitabe no zenmenkashika wo mezashite*.

Distributed in the United States by Kodansha America, LLC, and in the United Kingdom and continental Europe by Kodansha Europe Ltd.

Published by Kodansha International Ltd., 17–14 Otowa 1-chome, Bunkyo-ku, Tokyo 112–8652.

ISBN 978–4–7700–3163–1

First edition, 2011
19 18 17 16 15 14 13 12 11   10 9 8 7 6 5 4 3 2 1

Library of Congress Cataloging-in-Publication Data

880-01 Ezoe, Hiromasa, 1936-
[880-02 Torishirabe no "zenmen kashika" o mezashite. English]
Still seeking justice : reform and redress of Japan's flawed judicial system / compiled by Hiromasa Ezoe. -- 1st ed.
p. cm.
ISBN 978-4-7700-3163-1
1. Criminal justice, Administration of--Japan. 2. Lay judges--Japan. 3. 880-03 Ezoe, Hiromasa, 1936---Trials, litigation, etc. 4. 880-04 Rikuruto, Kabushiki Kaisha--Corrupt practices. I. Title.
KNX470.E9613 2011
345.52'05--dc22
2011003420

www.kodansha-intl.com

CONTENTS

Preface

Every year the members of my education class at the university hold a reunion. Spouses are welcome, of course. Unless circumstances prevented me from attending, I have always attended these gatherings.

At one such reunion, I ran into a classmate whom I had not seen in forty years and who had recently retired as a judge. While he was on the bench, he told me, he hadn't been able to attend events like this where alcohol was served. "And it's only now that I'm retired that I'm able to see my old acquaintances. I couldn't be happier." He added that the whole time he served as a judge he had lived in a government apartment and that as a rule he was not to socialize with anyone except other judges.

Our conversation continued, and gradually the former judge shifted the topic to the Recruit scandal. "I was very interested in your case and always kept abreast of developments in the press," he said. "I was sure you'd have to serve time. You're lucky to have gotten a suspended sentence."

This came as a surprise to me, as almost all my classmates who had followed careers in business and were aware of the issues at stake in the trial had told me they believed a suspended sentence would be fair and appropriate. This gap in perception was marked, and it brought home to me how different are the standards brought to bear by judges and by the average layman. That judges are forced to live in a narrow world, isolated from society, had to have something to do with this.

It was from encounters like this that I have come to believe that a lay judge system, where ordinary citizens—"a jury of one's peers," in American parlance—participate in trial proceedings, would have significant positive effect on Japanese justice.

For what is commonly referred to as the Recruit scandal, I had been put through the longest trial—thirteen years!—with the most court sessions in Japan's postwar history. It was worthy of a place in the *Guinness Book of World Records*. This is not something I am pleased to boast about. On the contrary, surely a trial that is dragged out that long does not serve the cause of justice either.

Unfortunately, however, the reforms currently underway in Japan, while a start in the right direction, are beset by a multitude of difficulties.

This book has been written as a companion volume to *Where Is the Justice?: Media Attacks, Prosecutorial Abuse, and My 13 Years in Japanese Court*, which I wrote and published a year ago. It is comprised of disparate chapters written by several of my defense attorneys and myself addressing what we see to be problems both in the ruling handed down in my trial and in the newly launched lay judge trial system. It is an attempt to contribute to the dialogue to improve a far-too-imperfect situation.

Prior to the actual writing, the contributors to this volume did not meet and discuss specific topics, nor did we make any effort to coordinate our various chapters.

This was deliberate, so as to present what we individually thought to be the most pressing concerns. The perspectives and content presented are thus quite diverse. Some of the observations are from many years of legal work; some are based on experience in the courtroom. My chapter was based on my personal experience.

The lay judge system has been in effect only a short time, but criticisms have been widespread—by people involved in the system, by social pundits, as well as by the wider legal community.

The lay judge system is slated to come up for review after three years. While at first glance this book might appear to be a mélange of topics, its underlying goal is the hope that it will serve as an aid and point of reference when that review is conducted.

HIROMASA EZOE
November 2010

I

WHY THE RECRUIT TRIAL TOOK SO LONG

The Need for Full Recording of Interrogations

Takeshi Tada, Attorney at Law

In August 2009 Japan launched a new system whereby citizens serve as lay judges in criminal trials. In the trials conducted under this new system to date, verdicts have been passed down and the trials brought to conclusion with remarkable swiftness—after just three or four days of deliberations.

In contrast, the criminal trial of Hiromasa Ezoe in the Recruit scandal (on charges of bribe passing), in which I served as a defense lawyer, spanned a period of over thirteen years and 322 court sessions. Along the way, the judges and prosecutors changed any number of times, but during the entire trial—from the pre-indictment investigation phase to the handing down of the verdict—I was a member of the defense team and attended every session in court. The final chapter of my life as an attorney was written almost entirely by the Recruit scandal—and tense days they were. When the court finally confirmed a suspended sentence against Mr. Ezoe, I felt that an enormous weight was lifted, and I experienced a sense of relief to the depths of my soul. A lengthy trial takes a major toll not only on the defendant, as one would expect, but on his lawyers as well. Obviously this is no way for justice to be carried out.

Mr. Ezoe's trial dragged on for so long for a number of reasons. First, the charges filed against him were numerous. He was indicted on eight counts of bribe passing through what was described as four "routes": members of the political world, the Labor Ministry, the Education Ministry, and

NTT (Nippon Telegraph and Telephone). Second, major battles were waged concerning just how "voluntary" Mr. Ezoe's confessions were and the "credibility" of written statements taken from case witnesses. Under Japan's Code of Criminal Procedure, any confession whose voluntariness is questionable—that is, when there is reasonable doubt as to whether it was extracted under coercion, torture, threat, etc.—cannot serve as evidence in court. The Code also prohibits the admission as evidence of statements taken from witnesses during the investigation phase unless there are special circumstances strongly supporting their credibility.

In the Recruit case, strong doubts existed about the legality and propriety of the prosecutors in their interrogations of Mr. Ezoe. Allegations flew that the prosecutors had made Mr. Ezoe stand for long periods facing the wall, made him kneel on the ground and beg for mercy, and baited him with offers of an early release on bail if he confessed to the charges against him. Accusations were also lodged that the prosecutors had coerced witnesses into making confessions against their will by subjecting them to relentless interrogations that continued well into the wee hours.

The fact that interrogations are carried out behind closed doors, away from open scrutiny, makes it easy for prosecutors to resort to unlawful means like coercion, physical abuse, and threats or leading questions. Through such unlawful tactics, they are able to elicit false confessions and written statements that have no basis in fact. Two recent cases that have received wide media coverage are the "Ashikaga case"—in which the accused was convicted of the kidnapping and murder of a young girl in 1990, only to have the original DNA evidence against him thrown out in 2009 and a retrial ordered (in which he was found innocent)—and the "Shibushi case"—in which twelve defendants were found guilty of vote buying in a local election, only to have the verdict overturned in 2007 because of the questionable methods used to force their original confessions. These are just two of any number of cases in which the voluntary nature and/or credibility of original written statements by indicted individuals have subsequently been rejected.

In Mr. Ezoe's trial, the prosecutors asked to have a huge number of written statements—upward of a thousand—admitted as evidence. The defense team of course alleged that the vast bulk of those statements had been wrested by the prosecutors through unlawful or improper methods, and we refused to agree to the prosecution's request. As a result, the prosecutors were compelled to demonstrate that the statements were reliable and had been taken voluntarily, and to do so they repeatedly called witnesses as well as the defendant and subjected them to questioning. I would estimate that more than seventy percent of the entire trial time was spent doing this.

Under the new trial system using lay judges, because the courts are not authorized to detain these private citizens at length, protracted trials are not permitted. Since disputes over the voluntariness and credibility of written statements have been a major cause of the dragging-out of trials, to achieve swift execution of trial proceedings the prosecution is now compelled to submit as evidence only those written statements whose voluntary nature and credibility can be proven. This can be achieved in one way only—by video-recording the entire interrogation process—that is, by making an audio-visual record of the circumstances that led a defendant to confess or that induced a witness to state facts disadvantageous to the defendant. When evidence in the form of such records is examined in court and its voluntariness and credibility are thus proven, there is no longer a need to question the defendant or witness on the points concerned. Recording interrogations on video makes it impossible for investigators to conduct unlawful or improper interrogations. Clearly, such recording serves as a deterrent to unlawful or improper interrogations and can contribute significantly to the execution of expeditious trial proceedings.

Had video recording been in place in the Recruit case, the trial could never have dragged out in excess of thirteen long years—and perhaps the indictments themselves may have never taken place. From my experience with the Recruit case, I am of the strong conviction that video recording of interrogations is a matter of utmost urgency for this nation's criminal trials.

The Supreme Public Prosecutors Office has issued guidelines pursuant to cases involving trial by lay judges, calling for audio and video recording— at the prosecution's discretion and responsibility—of such parts of the interrogations of the accused that are deemed appropriate, within a scope so as not to detract from the inherent function of the interrogation. Today, in accordance with those guidelines, partial recording of interrogations is undertaken.

The guidelines themselves are only of limited merit, however, as they apply solely to cases of serious crime that are subject to trial by lay judges. Instances when the voluntariness and credibility of an interrogation are disputed are not limited to cases involving serious offenses. There are many cases when an interrogation's voluntary nature and credibility are disputed, such as those involving bribe passing, where the awareness of the accused is a major point of contention. As such, video recording of interrogations is needed even in cases that do not call for a trial by lay judges.

It is also odd to limit audio and video recording to interrogations of accused parties alone. It is not only in reference to defendants' statements of confession that voluntariness and credibility constitute a point of contention. In cases involving alleged bribe passing, for example, where there is a need to establish background circumstances, numerous written statements by witnesses other than the defendant are submitted as evidence, and their credibility becomes a major point of dispute. In the Recruit trial, this was often the situation, demonstrating why video recording should not be limited to interrogations of accused parties.

The guidelines of the Supreme Public Prosecutors Office are premised on partial recording of interrogations; but with recording of only parts of interrogations, it is unclear what circumstances led to the accused giving his confession or to a witness making a statement of disadvantageous facts. Moreover, as it is left to the discretion of the prosecutor to decide which parts of the interrogation shall be recorded, the prosecutor is granted license to record only those parts that serve to his own advantage.

In the initial phase of his interrogations, Mr. Ezoe denied any intent of bribery concerning all "routes" in question. But as his detention grew protracted and he was subjected to the relentless interrogations marked by coercion, leading questions, and bargaining (what Mr. Ezoe said the prosecutors called "negotiations"), ultimately he was driven to sign statements of confession. For this reason, if interrogations are to be video-recorded, the undertaking is meaningless unless full recording of the entire interrogation process is carried out. Clearly, partial recording has no value as evidence demonstrating the voluntary nature and credibility of what emerges from interrogations.

As video recording of interrogations is still in the trial phase, understandably a variety of difficult issues must be resolved before it can be implemented fully. Nonetheless, video recording is an indispensable means for deterring unlawful or improper investigations and realizing swift court trials. As an attorney who suffered grievously from the protracted trial in the Recruit case, I join the call most earnestly for early implementation of full video recording of interrogations.

Takeshi Tada. Born in 1935. Graduated from Chuo University, Faculty of Law, passed the bar exam, 1957. Entered Legal Training and Research Institute of Japan, became Attorney at Law, registered with the Dai-ni Tokyo Bar Association, 1970. Established Tada Law Office, 1996.

Has served as vice chairman of the Dai-ni Tokyo Bar Association; instructor in criminal defense at the Legal Training and Research Institute of Japan, chairman of the Legal Apprentice Training Committee, among others.

II

THE RECRUIT TRIAL: TWO RULINGS

Shozaburo Ishida, Attorney at Law

On March 4, 2003, a verdict was handed down in the case against Hiromasa Ezoe—over thirteen years after his trial began.

With that verdict, one of the longest criminal trials in Japanese history, and one of the largest cases of its kind, finally came to a close. The trial had entailed 322 court sessions, interrogations of more than 130 witnesses, and in excess of one hundred thousand pages of court records.

The night before the verdict was handed down, I lodged, along with Mr. Ezoe, attorney Masanori Ono, and others on the defense team, at the Hotel New Otani. It was a tense wait. Even if a total not-guilty verdict was unlikely, we were hopeful that Mr. Ezoe might be found innocent of some of the charges against him. In the event that he were found guilty, however, would he be given a suspended sentence? The prosecutors were asking for four years of incarceration; they clearly were looking for the defendant to serve time. If the ruling called for imprisonment, it would be necessary to undertake procedures to win Mr. Ezoe's release on bail again. Discussions had already been held with the court to deal with that contingency.

Early the next morning we went to Mr. Ezoe's offices at the Ezoe Scholarship Foundation. Outside the building, TV camera crews were standing by in wait. At nine-thirty, we joined the defense team in front of the courthouse. As we entered the courtroom, cameras flashed at our every move. Kyuzaburo Hino, head of the defense team, was in attendance for the first time in a long while. Osamu Ishihara, a member of the team, was carrying

a huge briefcase; in it was cash for additional bail in the event of an unsuspended sentence.

At precisely ten o'clock, the three judges entered the courtroom. The
presiding judge, Megumi Yamamuro, seemed tense. "Will the defendant
please come forward," he began. "The court will now rule on the bribery charge against you for violating the Nippon Telegraph and Telephone
Corporation Law."

I don't know if it was Judge Yamamuro's style to address defendants in
the familiar *kimi*, an informal appellation for "you," but that was how he
spoke to Mr. Ezoe. "The court sentences the defendant to three years in
prison," the judge announced.

The prosecutors had asked for four. But the question remained: would
the sentence be suspended? After a pause, the judge proceeded to read the
judgment summary to the courtroom. Intently, with mixed feelings—a
sense of chagrin, or perhaps relief—I listened as Mr. Ezoe was pronounced
guilty on all counts . . . with a suspended sentence.

The Recruit scandal was a case in which Hiromasa Ezoe and others were
indicted on charges of passing or accepting bribes in the form of pre-flotation
shares of Recruit Cosmos, a real estate subsidiary of Recruit Co., Ltd., the
information magazine publishing giant founded by Mr. Ezoe. Among those
accused of accepting the shares were Chief Cabinet Secretary Takao Fujinami (the "Fujinami route"), lawmaker Katsuya Ikeda (the "Ikeda route"),
Labor Vice Minister Takashi Kato (the "Ministry of Labor route"), Education Vice Minister Kunio Takaishi (the "Ministry of Education route"), and
Chairman of NTT Hisashi Shinto (the "NTT route"). The trial centered on
a number of disputed contentions. Did the sale of pre-listed Recruit Cosmos
shares to these individuals constitute bribery? Were the shares transferred in
exchange for receiving favors of some kind? Did the transfers have anything
to do with these individuals' performance of their professional duties? Had
Ezoe personally been involved in the selling of the shares?

The main focus, however, was whether the provision of shares and the
political donations to Fujinami constituted bribery. The question revolved

around whether Ezoe had asked favors of Fujinami and then sold him the Recruit Cosmos shares as a token of his appreciation. Concerning this question, the court had already handed down two completely divergent rulings. Initially Ezoe and Fujinami had been tried together, but because Ezoe was on trial for passing bribes not only via the "Fujinami route" but via other routes as well, the proceedings against Fujinami were separated. On September 27, 1994, a ruling was handed down in District Court by presiding judge Hideaki Mikami (the "Mikami ruling"), finding Fujinami not guilty. The court concluded that the evidence did not demonstrate that Ezoe had asked Fujinami for any favors, and accordingly the sale of the shares and the donations did not constitute bribes, nor had Fujinami considered them to be bribes.

In contrast, in the proceedings against Ezoe, the court accepted the prosecution's contentions in their entirety and on March 4, 2003, found against Ezoe (the "Yamamuro ruling").

Both conclusions were reached through investigations conducted in the same courtroom, relying on the same evidence. To understand how such a thing could occur, some background is helpful:

Transfer of Recruit Cosmos Shares

In mid-September 1986, Ezoe telephoned the office of Chief Cabinet Secretary Fujinami. The person who answered the phone was Fujinami's secretary, Eiji Tokuda.

Ezoe explained that Recruit Cosmos's stock would soon be registered on the Over-the-Counter (OTC) market, and he was eager that Fujinami as well as Tokuda should hold some of these shares. Ezoe indicated that ten thousand shares had been prepared for Fujinami and two thousand shares for Tokuda, and Ezoe said the details would be handled by "Ono."

Toshihiro Ono, who was No. 2 among the Recruit president's secretaries, then proceeded to visit Tokuda and undertake the procedures necessary for the transfer of shares.

The shares were all in Tokuda's name.

It was this transfer of shares, together with the donations that Recruit had been making to Fujinami prior to this time, that came under suspicion as having constituted bribes.

Ezoe-Fujinami Meeting

On March 15, 1984, Ezoe, accompanied by his chief secretary, Masao Tatsumi, visited Fujinami at his official residence. They were seen off at the Recruit Building by Hitoshi Kashiwaki and others, traveling in the president's company car, reaching Fujinami's residence a little after eight a.m. Although it was mid-March, at that hour it was quite cold.

At the entrance hall they were greeted by a person who appeared to be Fujinami's assistant. He offered the visitors slippers and ushered them in to meet Fujinami, who was waiting for their arrival.

After pleasantries were exchanged, Ezoe spoke of how the private sector was not honoring the gentlemen's agreement regarding the time period for recruitment of graduating university students, and that the reason was that the civil service exam was being held too early in the year. This impacted the interests of Recruit, which published magazines listing up-to-the-minute employment opportunities. Ezoe went on to say that the private sector in fact preferred the civil service exam date be scheduled after the private sector had completed its recruitment. If that were the case, companies would not feel such urgency to recruit the brightest prospects with such haste, giving students truly interested in a civil service career the chance to concentrate on the exam. Ezoe asked Fujinami where he might go to discuss the matter and what approach he should take. Fujinami did not seem particularly interested, suggesting only that the matter should be discussed with appropriate parties in the National Personnel Authority.

The conversation was extremely short, lasting about ten minutes.

Asking for Favors?

According to the prosecution, it was at this meeting that the "asking for favors" had occurred. This was the "Fujinami route."

The prosecution's case was built around Ezoe's telling Fujinami that one reason the gentlemen's agreement wasn't being honored was because the national administrative institutions did not comply with the purport of the gentlemen's agreement insofar as the hiring of public servants was concerned. The prosecution contended that Ezoe had asked Fujinami to do whatever he could to see that a proper response was made in line with the agreement's purport. The transfer of shares was Ezoe's way of thanking Fujinami for his efforts.

Bribery stands as a crime when a request is made of a public servant or individual in an official position and something is provided as an expression of thanks.

In Japanese society, the Recruit case was a major scandal. The case was by no means simple. The "Fujinami route" alone was fraught with a variety of questionable points. What favors had been asked for? Had the transfer of shares and other gifts been in gratitude for such favors, as commensurate compensation? Had the donations been made partly as a token of appreciation for the favors?

The Recruit scandal does not have a simple plot as in the Lockheed scandal of the 1970s, when five hundred million yen was provided in return for the prime minister's using his influence to induce All Nippon Airways to adopt the TriStar aircraft. The biggest point of contention in this case was whether Ezoe had asked for favors from Fujinami in his official position as the chief cabinet secretary.

Ezoe made personal contact with Fujinami on this one occasion only— on March 15, 1984. So the foremost issue was the content of the conversation that took place on that day and the outcome the conversation had brought about.

The Gentlemen's Agreement and the Schedule for the Civil Service Exam

At this meeting, Ezoe spoke with Fujinami about the gentlemen's agreement on hiring and the timing of the examination for upper-level civil servants.

The gentlemen's agreement, which was dispensed with in 1997, was an understanding between universities and companies that only after a specified date would companies have any contact with students with regards to possible employment. The agreement, it was said, had two purposes. On the one hand, it ensured students an uninterrupted environment for study during their senior year, it helped to level the playing field for students seeking jobs, and it guaranteed students equal opportunity in job seeking. And on the other hand, it afforded companies an orderly hiring process.

The Ad Hoc Council on Education, in its first report in 1985, saw the agreement as a way of mitigating the ills inherent in the nation's inordinate emphasis on academic credentials. The council recommended that both the corporate and public sectors should end their practice of early hiring, which was in violation of the agreement and which led to unbalanced hiring of students from better known schools.

In 1983, the agreement in place was the "October-November agreement"; that is, October 1st was the first date that students could visit companies to learn of employment possibilities, and November 1st was the first date that companies could conduct interviews and start their selection process. The public sector, however, followed a different timetable. Preliminary national civil service exams would have taken place on July 3rd; follow-up interviews and testing would have been conducted during August 3rd–19th; and the list of successful candidates would have been announced on October 15th.

Thus, students who had sat for the civil service exam found themselves in a quandary. They would not learn the results until October 15th, and would not know whether to make the rounds of the private companies beginning on October 1st. This situation also brought with it the unsettling possibility that students who might have passed the civil service exam would visit companies and accept a job offer, causing public agencies to lose outstanding talent to the private sector. To rectify this situation, public agencies sought an earlier date on which the civil service exam results would be announced so as to give the public sector an equal chance to secure outstanding talent and simultaneously relieve students from agonizing over the choice between the public and private sector.

This was the position taken by the National Personnel Authority (NPA), and in early 1983, it made a proposal to that effect to the Japan Federation of Employers' Associations (Nikkeiren), which was in a leadership position within the Central Employment Measures Council, an organization comprised of companies seeking to recruit employees, that was party to the gentlemen's agreement. The Nikkeiren, however, rejected the proposal, fearing that if the results of the civil service exam were announced earlier, some companies might dare not to honor the gentlemen's agreement at all. No changes were therefore made to the timetable.

In 1984, the NPA appealed to the Nikkeiren once again, requesting that the date for announcing the civil service exam results be made earlier. It was around this time that Ezoe visited Fujinami at his official residence.

Ezoe's Thinking

What concerned Ezoe was that the gentlemen's agreement was gradually being abrogated by the private sector. The reason, he believed, was the timing of the civil service exam. Although the results of the exam would not be announced before October 15th, contact between students and government agencies actually would have taken place before the October 1st date when students could begin to visit private companies. The public sector thus had an unfair advantage. Under the circumstances, the private sector, equally eager to hire outstanding talent, could not stand idly by, and it began to seek contact with students before October 1st.

Ezoe reasoned that in order to resolve the situation, the civil service interview exam needed to be administered after October 1st. This would put the private sector on an equal footing with the public sector in its recruitment of students. It was with this in mind that Ezoe went to see Fujinami. While the scheduling of civil service exams was outside the prerogative of the chief cabinet secretary, Ezoe sought his advice as to whom he might plead his case concerning this matter.

The "Matsuzaki Memo"

Upon taking his leave from Fujinami's residence, Ezoe went directly to meet with Yoshinobu Matsuzaki, the senior managing director of the Nikkeiren. Matsuzaki was the person in charge of the gentlemen's agreement from the hiring side.

What Ezoe spoke of on that occasion was written up by Matsuzaki in a memo to be passed on to Kazuo Inoue, the officer in charge of employment at the Nikkeiren.

> *Mr. Ezoe thinks it would work well if August 3–19 were shifted to after October 1st. He said Mr. Fujinami replied he would consider it if a petition were submitted by an appropriate source.*

In handing down his ruling, Judge Mikami found that the purport of the memo was this: "It reported that in order for the gentlemen's agreement to be honored, [Ezoe] thought the civil service exam should be pushed back until after October 1st; but when he presented his argument to the defendant [Fujinami], the defendant replied he would consider the matter if a petition were to come from an appropriate source."

Moving the Announcement of the Results Forward

The situation shifted, however, and instead of pushing back the exam date, the issue moved in the direction of bringing the results announcement date forward, as the public agencies wanted.

When the National Personnel Authority requested that the results of the 1984 civil service exam be announced on October 1st, Inoue of the Nikkeiren expressed the view that the shift would be unavoidable, so long as the public agencies pledged to honor the intent of the gentlemen's agreement.

In response, the NPA began laying the groundwork for getting the Nikkeiren and other economic organizations to agree to moving forward the date for announcing the results of the civil service exam. Specifically the NPA sought to get a pledge from the public agencies to honor the gentlemen's agreement with the private sector at meetings of the officers in charge of personnel matters at the various agencies, which were venues for discussions among the officers who oversee hiring at the agencies.

In order to secure such a pledge, on March 9, 1984, the officer in charge of planning at the NPA's Bureau of Recruitment, together with Cabinet Counselor Toru Nakamura, who presided at meetings of personnel chiefs in the government agencies, as well as the personnel officers at the Ministry of Finance and Ministry of International Trade and Industry—which were in strong competition with the industrial sector vis-à-vis student hiring—met with Inoue, who was the Nikkeiren's man in charge of the gentlemen's agreement, and engaged in an exchange of opinions. On March 16th, these same individuals then met with key officers in the three main economic organizations—the Nikkeiren, the Japan Chamber of Commerce and Industry (JCCI), and the National Federation of Small Business Associations (NFSBA). As a result of these meetings, a basic understanding was reached for moving forward the date for announcing the results of the civil service exam on the condition that the parties pledged to honor the gentlemen's agreement.

After going through this process, on March 21th, the head of the NPA's Bureau of Recruitment, Shigeharu Kagoshima, met with Matsuzaki. The two reached an agreement of cooperation whereby, in exchange for moving forward the date for announcing the civil service exam results, the gentlemen's agreement would be honored with respect to hiring of civil servants.

Consequent to this, the officer in charge of planning at the NPA's Bureau of Recruitment, a subordinate of Kagoshima's, met on March 28th with members of the Central Employment Measures Council and won their approval to move forward the date of the results of the civil service exam. The same day, at a meeting of personnel officers of various government agencies, agreement was reached, in accordance with the NPA's view, to cooperate with the gentlemen's agreement and to respect the intent of the agreement as regards visits by students to "old boys" (graduates of their particular universities) before October 1st and visits to the government agencies after October 1st—with the understanding that the corporate sector would commence their selections on November 1st.

The Prosecution's Scenario

The prosecution contended that when Ezoe met with Fujinami, in addition to asking that the civil service exam schedule be pushed back, he requested a ban on contact between government agencies and students before October 1st. In their indictment, this was referred to as "steps to prevent early recruitment of civil servants," and the scenario written by the prosecutors was that the agreement by personnel officers was realized as a result of Ezoe's having made such a request of Fujinami.

False Scenario

By no means, however, was this other issue on Ezoe's mind.

Ezoe's fundamental thinking was that unless a specific system—and not a concept like an "agreement"—were created to accord with the private sector's gentlemen's agreement as regards the hiring of upper-level civil servants, it would not carry the weight to ensure adherence. An "agreement" to prevent early recruitment—that is, to respect the purport of the gentlemen's agreement—had been in effect by government agencies earlier than 1984, but had proved ineffective. Ezoe had no interest in another such "agreement."

One way to resolve the problem, Ezoe believed, was to push back the schedule of the interviews for upper-level civil servant positions. This was identical in nuance to students' pushing back their visits to companies in the private sector. Other than to bring up the issue of the timetable of tests, Ezoe would have no reason to request something as obscure as taking "steps to prevent the early recruitment of civil servants."

Ezoe related these matters in detail at his trial.

Fujinami, too, never instructed anyone concerned to make any agreements.

The "agreement," as noted above, was reached as a result of negotiations between the NPA and three economic organizations. It had absolutely no connection to Ezoe's visit to Fujinami.

The Mikami and Yamamuro Rulings

As to whether or not Ezoe requested that Fujinami take "steps to prevent the early recruitment of civil servants," the verdicts reached by Judges Mikami and Yamamuro were completely opposite of one another.

The Mikami ruling is as follows:

> *Ezoe, thinking it desirable to push back the civil service exam schedule in order to force adherence to the gentlemen's agreement on hiring, visited the defendant [Chief Cabinet Secretary Fujinami] at his official residence on March 15, 1984, and explained that a major reason why the private sector gentlemen's agreement on hiring was not being adhered to was the early hiring of civil servants. He contended that pushing back the civil service exam would be one way of preventing early recruitment of civil servants, and he asked what steps might possibly be taken to achieve this. As to whether Ezoe went beyond that in asking the defendant to prevent early recruitment by government agencies, reasonable doubt remains.*

By contrast, the concluding portion of the Yamamuro ruling reads thus:

> *Based on "the statements, deemed credible, made by the defendant [Ezoe] before the prosecutors," when the defendant visited Fujinami's official residence on March 15, 1984, the court finds that he requested Fujinami not only to push back the schedule for announcing the results of the civil service exam but also, because one of the reasons for the failure of private companies to adhere to the gentlemen's agreement is that the nation's administrative organizations do not honor the intent of the gentlemen's agreement with respect to hiring of civil servants, to do everything in his power to get the nation's administrative institutions to make appropriate response in line with the purport of the gentlemen's agreement.*

The difference between these rulings is fundamental. The question is whether Ezoe asked Fujinami to, as described in the Mikami ruling, "prevent the early recruitment of civil servants" or, as explained in the Yamamuro ruling, "get the nation's administrative institutions to make appropriate response in line with the purport of the gentlemen's agreement."

What complicates establishment of the facts here is that the Mikami ruling also states that it is absolutely certain that preventing early recruitment by government agencies was a topic discussed between Ezoe and Fujinami. Yet, the Mikami ruling found the defendant not guilty because, it said, the topic was broached by Ezoe as a prelude to discussing steps for pushing back the civil service exam schedule. Therefore, there was reasonable doubt as to whether Ezoe had any intent beyond that to ask for specific favors relating to steps to prevent early recruitment by government agencies.

In other words, the Mikami ruling found that Ezoe thought bringing forward the announcement of the civil service exam results and the attendant "agreement" were inadequate to prevent early hiring by the government agencies, and he actually saw pushing back the civil service exam schedule as a favorable measure. And wishing to see the latter realized, he had merely brought up the matter with Fujinami, asking him where he might go and what approach he should take to achieve this.

The Yamamuro ruling, on the other hand, said that the court findings were that around March 13, 1984, Ezoe, having concluded that he could not approve of moves to bring forward the announcement of the civil service exam results, had it in mind to push back the civil service exam schedule and to prevent early recruitment by the government agencies by prohibiting contact with students by government agencies before October 1st. And so, the ruling said, Ezoe had decided to approach the chief cabinet secretary to achieve those ends. The court thus ruled that Ezoe's visit to Fujinami had been an act undertaken in order to bring about an "agreement."

Even as the various points that led to these conclusions are in dispute, the judgments differ. How could such opposing conclusions be drawn from the same evidence? The reason, close examination reveals, would seem to be in the way Ezoe's written statements as drawn up by the prosecutors were regarded. For example, on April 30, 1989, there is record of Ezoe having made the following statement as prepared by prosecutors:

> *In February or March of 1984 or 1985, I visited Chief Cabinet Secretary Fujinami at his official residence and requested that steps be taken with regard to early recruitment of civil servants. "The problem of early recruitment of civil servants is a major reason why the gentlemen's agreement on hiring is not being honored," I said, "and it's also become a social issue. Isn't there something that can be done about this? It's a case of the public sector being given preferential treatment over the private sector, and I'd like to see the public side do what would be proper. Isn't there anything that can be done about the early recruitment of civil servants?" I also said, "Would it be possible also to do something about pushing back the timing of the announcement of the results of the civil service exam?" and I asked where I should go and how I should go about making such a request. Mr. Fujinami replied, "I'm not familiar with the details of the civil service exam or any announcement of the results, but it isn't acceptable for the public side alone to be hiring people in advance, is it? I'll look into it and try to find out what it's all about, including where and how such decisions are made. Let me think about this problem of early recruitment by the public agencies."*

Again, on May 14, 1989, prosecutors have prepared this written statement for Ezoe:

> *In March 1984, I visited Fujinami at his official residence and requested that, in his position as chief cabinet secretary, he take steps of some sort to prevent the early recruitment of civil servants. "The reason I've come to see you today is that, despite the existence of the Ministry of Education's directive on the job-seeking activities of*

*university students and agreements like the understanding with the
Central Employment Measures Council, the government agencies
pay no heed to such things and make their hiring decisions early. This
early recruitment of civil servants is a major reason why the private
sector's gentlemen's agreement isn't being honored, creating a social
issue and making lots of problems for us, too. Isn't there something
that could be done about this? The public sector is being given pref-
erential treatment over the private sector, and we'd like to see the
public side do what's proper. Please, couldn't you do something to
prevent this early recruitment of civil servants?" "I'll give the matter some thought," Mr. Fujinami replied. As regards my speaking
with Mr. Fujinami about the issue of pushing back the schedule for
announcing the results of the civil service exam, this is as I stated in
my previous statement."*

Then again, the prosecutor's statement of May 19, 1989, contains a
record to the following effect:

*In mid-March 1984, I visited Chief Cabinet Secretary Fujinami at
his official residence and requested that steps be taken to prevent the
early recruitment of civil servants. He said he would think the matter
over.*

At their face value, the claims as composed by the prosecution were correct and acknowledged by Ezoe; that is, he states that he did ask Fujinami
to "take steps to prevent the early recruitment of civil servants." The problem is whether these statements of Ezoe's as written by the prosecution can
be believed. During his trial Ezoe contended repeatedly that he had been
forced to sign these statements against his will, and that what he was saying in the court was what was correct.

Against those claims, the Yamamuro ruling said that the content of
the prosecution's statements was more credible than Ezoe's statements in
court.

The Mikami ruling said the prosecution's statements were not credible.

In a nutshell, the difference between these two judgments likely has to do with the fundamental approach to the prosecution's statements: Are they to be read with skepticism from the outset? Or does one assume their credibility from the start? Depending on one's approach, major differences can occur in how one views and treats objective as well as peripheral evidence.

The Meaning of the "Matsuzaki Memo"

First, there is the matter of Ezoe's visit to Yoshinobu Matsuzaki, the senior managing director of the Nikkeiren, and the meaning of the "Matsuzaki memo."

The Mikami ruling states:

> *According to the record saying, "I was told that Mr. Ezoe thinks everything would go well if August 3rd–19th were changed to after October 1st, and Mr. Fujinami replied that he would consider the matter if a petition were to come from an appropriate source"; and what Matsuzaki stated before the court, that on March 15, 1984, Mr. Ezoe visited Matsuzaki at the Nikkeiren and reported that when he appealed to the defendant [Chief Cabinet Secretary Fujinami] that he believed that in order for the gentlemen's agreement to be honored the civil service exam schedule should be pushed back to after October 1st, the defendant had responded that he would consider the matter if a petition were to come from an appropriate source. However, the report in fact made no mention whatsoever concerning preventing contact between the government agencies and students before October 1st.*

Since no mention whatsoever was made about prohibiting contact between the government agencies and students before October 1st, the Mikami ruling concludes that no such conversation took place, making it clear that the Matsuzaki memo was treated as an important piece of evidence corroborating that what Ezoe and Fujinami had talked about was largely "pushing back the civil service exam schedule."

The Yamamuro ruling, on the other hand, states that the Matsuzaki memo was not necessarily a record of everything Matsuzaki was told by Ezoe. It concludes that in Ezoe's conversation with Matsuzaki, it is conceivable that Ezoe may not have touched upon the matter of preventing early recruitment by the government agencies—something originally demanded by the corporate sector. It concludes that even though there is no record of their having discussed the matter, the possibility of their having discussed the matter cannot be excluded. In other words, the Matsuzaki memo is not a record of everything that was discussed in the conversation, and it is conceivable, the ruling said, that no written mention was made of their discussing the matter of preventing early recruitment.

Which makes more sense? The Mikami ruling, which takes the Matsuzaki memo at face value and says it does not contradict what Ezoe stated in his trial?

Or the Yamamuro ruling, which assumes the possibility a discussion took place concerning "prohibiting contact between government agencies and students before October 1st" that was not recorded in the memo?

Without this assumption, Judge Yamamuro would have been unable to reject Ezoe's statements in court and would have had to find the record contained in the prosecution's statements to be correct. What the judge aimed to do here is, based on the presupposition that the record of the written statements is correct, to treat objective evidence through speculative eyes.

In this manner, the Yamamuro ruling does not sound convincing, as it had to affirm the credibility of the prosecution's statements by infusing speculation to the defendant's disadvantage and without treating objective evidence at face value.

Subsequent to Ezoe's visit to his official residence, Fujinami made inquiries about bringing forward the date for announcing the results of the civil

service exam to Shigeharu Kagoshima, head of the NPA's Bureau of Recruitment, and Cabinet Counselor Nakamura. On those occasions, he posed no
questions at all concerning prohibiting contact between the government
agencies and students before October 1st, or about any pledge agreed on at
the meetings of heads of personnel.

For their part, Kagoshima and Nakamura both stated that Chief Cabinet
Secretary Fujinami had made inquiries only regarding one point: bringing
forward the date for announcing the results of the civil service exam. This
would suggest that when Ezoe visited Fujinami at his official residence, he
had discussed the impending advancement of the date for announcing the
civil service exam results.

It would be also highly improbable that Ezoe would go out of his way
to visit Fujinami at his residence to request early recruitment by government agencies in the context of bringing forward the announcement of
the exam results in the light, especially, that at the time an agreement was
being reached between the NPA, Nikkeiren, and others on honoring the
gentlemen's agreement and prohibiting contact between the agencies and
students before October 1st as a precondition for bringing forward the
announcement of the exam results.

In this respect, the Mikami ruling concludes that it would have been reasonable for Ezoe to have explained to Fujinami about the advancement of
the date for announcing the civil service exam results, to have expressed his
sentiments about the problems that would create, and to have mentioned
that he had been wondering what steps might be taken to push back the
exam schedule—and that he thus discussed with Fujinami what he might
do to bring it about.

Statement of May 19th

A significant gap also exists between the two rulings concerning the circumstances behind the preparation of Ezoe's statement of May 19, 1989,
and their respective evaluations of it.

Before undertaking that day's interrogation, the prosecutor had prepared a new statement, taking a statement drawn up earlier as his reference, showed it to Ezoe, and had him make additions to it as he saw fit. As drawn up by the prosecutor, the statement read as follows concerning what took place when Ezoe visited Fujinami:

> *I requested of Chief Cabinet Secretary Fujinami that something be done to prevent the early recruitment of students to become civil servants, and also that the date for announcing the successful candidates of the civil service exam be pushed back.*

Ezoe, after reading it, altered it to read:

> *I requested that measures be taken to prevent the early recruitment of students to become civil servants—specifically, that the date for announcing the successful candidates of the civil service exam be pushed back.*

Here again, Ezoe attempted to clarify that what he "specifically" spoke about with Fujinami during his visit was the issue of pushing back the date for announcing the results of the civil service exam. Later, however, this portion of the text was deleted by the prosecutor, only to have Ezoe write "stet" to retain it. This exchange was repeated a second time, Ezoe making every attempt to leave his emendation in.

The prosecutor, thinking that doing so would conflict with the original statement, forcibly deleted this portion of the text.

As a result, the record simply read:

> *If memory serves me right, when I visited Chief Cabinet Secretary Fujinami at his official residence, I requested that measures be taken to prevent the early recruitment of students to become civil servants.*

The final statement thus neglects even to mention the objective fact that the two men discussed the matter of the civil service exam schedule.

The Mikami ruling makes a very shrewd observation concerning this point, acknowledging Ezoe's side of the story:

> *In the prosecution's statement dated May 19, 1989, there is no men-tion whatsoever concerning a request to have the schedule of the civil service exam pushed back—a request that has been objectively made clear; it deals wholly with the request about taking measures to pre-vent the early recruitment of civil servants. Furthermore, as recorded in the text drawn up by Prosecutor [Tamotsu] Shoji, there are traces indicating that, at least on one occasion, Ezoe tried to insert the word "specifically" between the passages "I requested . . . that something be done to prevent the early recruitment of students to become civil servants" and "[I] also [requested] that the date for announcing the successful candidates of the civil service exam be pushed back." From these facts, the doubt cannot be erased that, as Ezoe stated at his trial, the statement was drawn up against his will, with the prosecu-tor telling him that scheduling the civil service exam on the same day as [the date prescribed] in the gentlemen's agreement equated to the issue of the early recruitment of civil servants; and therefore the court cannot believe the content of these various statements by the prosecu-tion concerning this point.*

The Yamamuro ruling, on the other hand, held that the record as stated was correct. The judge opined that Ezoe's statements made in the court-room lacked substantiation and had meager credibility in view of the three points:

> *One, the statements in question made by the defendant during his trial are not based on specific memories but rather are based on specu-lation. Two, at the time of the interrogations in question, in his deten-tion cell the defendant was keeping a record of the circumstances of his interrogations in notebooks, and therefore if the circumstances as stated by the defendant were true, they would be recorded in those*

*notebooks; but while it would thus seem possible to substantiate his
statements in court by asking for the notebooks to be submitted as
evidence, the defendant has made no such request. Three, at the time
of the interrogations in question, the defense counsel was meeting
with the defendant for many hours almost daily, preparing reports
on the content of those meetings, and having those reports confirmed
and dated at a notary public's office; the report prepared on the result
of his meeting on the day following the date the statement in question was prepared contains only a record stating that Prosecutor
Shoji took out the statement he had already prepared, showed it to
the defendant, and the defendant, contending that it ran counter to
the facts, refused to sign it; when Prosecutor Shoji then pressed him,
asking him why he would not admit to what he had already admitted
to Prosecutor [Norio] Munakata, [the defendant] had no choice but
to sign; there is no record whatsoever to the effect that the defendant
added to or deleted from the original text and his revisions were not
allowed.*

The logic behind this Yamamuro ruling is very strange. All the ruling mentions is that what Ezoe stated at his trial was "speculation"; that
although it can be surmised he recorded the events in his notebooks, he did
not ask to have them submitted as evidence; and that he said nothing about
this during the meeting with his defense counsel. It completely neglects
what is most important: the objective fact that an emended text exists.

The fact that Ezoe was shown a statement prepared by the prosecutor
and made changes to it is fully proven by the objective existence of the
emended text shown in court. The prosecution itself admitted to the process by which the emendations were made.

The court brings up a totally different event and attempts to use it
to explain the credibility of the prosecution's statement. This is nothing
but irrational logic arising from a desire not to reject the credibility of the
prosecution's statements.

Follow-up Visit

Subsequent to Ezoe's visit to Fujinami, on March 24, 1984, Naotaka Ida—at the time, senior managing director at Recruit—and several others paid a visit to the chief cabinet secretary. The prosecution contended their visit was made in conjunction with Ezoe's having asked favors from Fujinami, the allegation being that they visited him to ask what had been done as a result of Ezoe's "requests." The matter is referred to as the "follow-up" issue.

On the date in question, Ida and the others arrived at 12:35 p.m. at the building where Diet members have their offices. The afternoon session of the Upper House Budget Committee meeting was to begin at 12:50, and Fujinami was there to answer questions at the start of the meeting.

The intervening time was fifteen minutes.

Ida and the others completed visitor registration procedures at the reception desk on the first floor and then proceeded to the third floor to see Fujinami. There, they greeted his secretary, an exchange of name cards was made, and the group then took an elevator down to the basement level where an underground corridor connects to the Diet Building. They then went up to the chief cabinet secretary's office on the second floor.

To walk from Fujinami's office in the office wing to his office in the Diet Building takes at least eight minutes. Adding in the time it took to register at the reception desk and then go to Fujinami's office upstairs, greet his secretary and exchange name cards, and considering the time at which Fujinami took his seat at the committee meeting, Ida's visit with him could have lasted no more than two or three minutes.

The venue of Ida and Fujinami's meeting was the chief cabinet secretary's office in the Diet Building. That office is adjacent to the office of the cabinet counselor, and the door separating the two is normally open, allowing free passage between the two offices. Given this time frame and location, it is altogether unthinkable that Ida could or would have discussed matters of the kind that the prosecution contended

On March 21st, three days before that meeting, Recruit had held a party at the Hotel New Otani to commemorate the change of the company name. Approximately 1,700 people had been invited to attend. The reason

Ida visited Fujinami was to express gratitude for his having attended the party.

The prosecution contended that given Fujinami's schedule on the date in question, his attendance at the party could not have been possible, and therefore Ida could not have visited him to thank him for having attended. The prosecution's logic was this: On the day in question, after the Upper House Budget Committee meeting finished at 6:13 p.m., Fujinami had attended a gathering in conjunction with Prime Minister Nakasone's impending visit to China at the prime minister's residence and after that he attended a meeting at Kakyotei, a restaurant in Akasaka. Under the circumstances, the prosecutors alleged, Fujinami could not have attended the Recruit party, and therefore Ida's visit could not have been made to thank him for attending.

The prosecution's contention is based on the assumption that on the day in question Fujinami proceeded through the day precisely on schedule, never being late for any of his appointments. That assumption itself was never proven.

Diet members frequently take time out of their tight schedules to put in brief appearances, making rounds of greetings, at parties like Recruit's. The distance between the Diet Building and the Hotel New Otani, where the Recruit party took place, takes only a few minutes by car. It is possible that after the Budget Committee meeting broke up at 6:13 p.m., Fujinami put in a brief appearance at the Recruit party, then went slightly late to the Nakasone affair at the prime minister's residence; or, after attending the Nakasone affair, he could have dropped by at the Recruit party, which went on until about 7:30, and then gone to the meeting at Kakyotei. Even if he arrived at either of those gatherings five or six minutes late, it is perfectly conceivable the impression would have been that he arrived on time.

According to Fujinami's diary, the gathering at Kakyotei was scheduled for 7:00. It was to be a meeting with journalists, however, and given its nature, the gathering did not necessarily have to begin precisely at that hour.

To go from the prime minister's residence to Kakyotei via the Hotel New Otani is not very far, and doing so takes just a few minutes. It is also altogether feasible time-wise that, after the Nakasone affair broke up a little after 7:00, Fujinami went from the prime minister's residence to the Recruit party, and from there proceeded directly to Kakyotei.

But more fundamentally, there was absolutely no need for Ida to pay such a "follow-up" visit to Fujinami on March 24th in the first place. By that point, in the wake of a trio of meetings—between the head of planning at the National Personnel Authority and Kazuo Inoue, the officer in charge of employment issues at the Nikkeiren, on March 9th; between the head of planning at the NPA and the three major economic organizations on March 16th; and between Shigeharu Kagoshima, head of the NPA's Bureau of Recruitment, and Matsuzaki, senior managing director of Nikkeiren, on March 21st—plans had already been set to bring forward the exam schedule and to reach an "understanding" in return for doing so.

Accordingly, on the eve of the meeting where that understanding was to come about, the situation did not call for, as the prosecution contended, any probing to see how Fujinami was responding to Ezoe's alleged request for favors and, if need be, to repeat that request. Especially after the aforementioned meeting of March 21st, there was absolutely no reason for anyone from Recruit to go to Fujinami on March 24th to collect new information or make any further pleas.

The Mikami and Yamamuro rulings also take polar opposite views toward this matter. The Mikami ruling says no follow-up visit took place, while the Yamamuro ruling says it did.

First, on the matter of where the visit occurred, the Mikami ruling has this to say:

It has been acknowledged that the offices of the chief cabinet secretary and the cabinet counselor are next to each other in the Diet Building, and that the door between them is generally kept open, allowing free passage between them. Accordingly, this would seem to be an inappropriate place for Mr. Ida and his two companions to seek confirmation from the defendant [Fujinami] of the outcome of Ezoe's request.

Meanwhile, the Yamamuro ruling offers the following opinion:

Since the intent was to confirm Fujinami's response to a request made several days earlier by the defendant [Ezoe] and not to ask for anything new, no time was needed to explain the situation, and the content of the meeting as stated by both parties could have been carried out in a short time, and for that reason both in terms of timing and location one cannot say it was inappropriate.

The prosecution contended that Ezoe went to Fujinami's official residence to ask "favors" of him early in the morning in order to avoid notice. If so, it would be highly unlikely that to learn the outcome of his request, he would send a third party—no less a party of three persons—on a rushed visit to a place where people would be coming and going freely. It must be said that the Mikami ruling, which focuses on Ezoe's statement that he gave no instructions that the visit take place to confirm the outcome of his supposed request for favors, and that if his intent had been to confirm such an outcome it would have sufficed for him to telephone Fujinami directly—there would be no need to send Ida and the others—is the view that hits the mark.

Second, concerning the Recruit party at the Hotel New Otani, the Mikami ruling comes to the following conclusion:

Judging from the fact that the Recruit party took place three days before the visit by Ida and his two colleagues to the defendant [Fujinami], in addition to the fact that Ida and the others met with the defendant in his office in the Diet Building only briefly immediately before he then went to respond to questioning in the Diet, it would not be altogether unnatural for Ida and the others to have visited the defendant in order to express appreciation for his having attended the Recruit party.

In contrast, the Yamamuro ruling comes to this conclusion:

The defense contends that after attending the affair in conjunction with the prime minister's visit to China, it is possible for Fujinami to have made a brief stop at the Recruit party and then proceeded to Kakyotei; however, it is difficult to conceive that the chief cabinet secretary, who would be serving as the prime minister's representative during his absence, would give his send-off speech and then swiftly take his leave without conversing with the prime minister and his staff. Moreover, by the time he finished his speech, the Recruit gathering would have already been nearing its scheduled end, and considering the time required to get there, he would have worried that the gathering would have already broken up, so it makes no sense that at that point he would think of attending an affair he had not planned on attending originally. Even supposing that Fujinami did consider the Recruit gathering important enough that he wanted to attend even if it would make him late to Kakyotei, he would have arranged his schedule that way from the outset; moreover, if he was to attend a party regardless of the inconvenience it would cause, one would expect he would have preference to the gathering for social activist Hideo Kato—an affair he helped organize—rather than the Recruit gathering to which he had merely been an invitee, but as noted above, Fujinami was absent from the gathering for Hideo Kato.

In this way, the Yamamuro ruling completely ignored the points the Mikami ruling had called into question.

Next was the matter of the lack of any internal documents. If Ida and the others had paid a follow-up visit to Fujinami, there should have been a report or other document of some sort hinting at this.

The Mikami ruling raises a question concerning this:

If Ida and the others had confirmed the outcome of [Ezoe's] requests to the defendant [Fujinami], one would expect there to be some record in documents at Recruit indicating a report of this; but in all the internal documents from Recruit submitted as evidence to this court dating from March 24, 1984, onward, there is no such record at all.

On this point too, the Yamamuro ruling employed logic based on speculation:

Since it was the director in charge of sales, the general sales manager, and the chief secretary of the president who visited Fujinami, there was no need for an internal report to superiors in the first place. Also, since it would have sufficed for Ida, the director in charge, or Ono, the No. 2 secretary, to report in person to the defendant [Ezoe], it is not unnatural for there to have been no document prepared reporting this; and even supposing such a document had been prepared, it could easily have been disposed of before the investigation started, and therefore the fact that such a document does not exist does not constitute a circumstance affecting the credibility of the various statements made during the investigation phase by Ida and Abe.

Political Donations

Ezoe's visit to Fujinami took place in March 1984, and he sold him the shares of Recruit Cosmos stock two-and-a-half years later, in September 1986. The prosecution, sensing that a scenario purporting that Ezoe expressed his appreciation this way after a lapse of two-and-a-half years would seem unusual, turned to the fact that during that interim Recruit had made political contributions to Fujinami, and it alleged that these too were bribes. The donations made by Recruit to Fujinami were recorded in the company's accounts. Likewise, on Fujinami's side the funds were also handled as political donations. The prosecution claimed those donations, altogether in compliance with the law, were bribes.

The prosecution's scenario was that in early August 1984, Ezoe, after visiting Fujinami the previous March, approached Fujinami with an offer of "bribes," which he proposed by saying that "for the time being" he would provide him with political donations in the amount of five million yen every half-year, that is to say, ten million yen each year.

In order for this scenario to hold water, the offer of such bribes would have had to be made after March 1984; otherwise it could not have been an expression of appreciation for having responded to his request. The fact of the matter, however, is that Recruit had already been making donations to Fujinami on a regular basis starting in 1982. Furthermore, in November 1983, a donation of five million yen had been made in the form of a check. In making the donation, Recruit had gone through the standard procedures required under the Political Funds Control Act.

The prosecution, however, made no mention of this during its interrogations and also made no attempt to bring this fact up in court. As a result, the donation of November 1983 does not appear anywhere in the written statements of Ezoe or anyone else who was involved.

The fact came to light for the first time when, in the course of court proceedings, it was submitted by the defense as evidence. When that happened, the prosecution made every attempt to conjure up a plausible argument. It stated that Fujinami's office maintained two separate accounts—one, a bank account for managing its funds; the other, a deposit account for membership fees collected from political groups and the like—and the ordinary deposit account into which the check had been deposited had been used as an account for receiving funds to support election activities. Accordingly, it claimed, the check in question had been provided on a one-time basis to support Fujinami's election effort, and therefore it differed in nature from the regular donations made between August 1984 and December 1985.

Granted, money conceivably to be used to support initiatives timed with elections had been deposited into this account. But at the same time the account had also received regular political donations and donations that had nothing to do with elections.

Moreover, the timing of the check transfer was late November. This is *seibo* season, when gifts are traditionally given and when regular political donations are made. Such donations are rendered in the form of checks, as was the case after 1984. That the check in question was deposited into this account was a matter largely decided by Fujinami's office, according to what would be most convenient; Recruit had no involvement in the decision. Subsequent to this, the company's checks were deposited into various accounts at various times. Appeals issued by the Kansai Shunju Kenkyukai, a group soliciting financial support for Fujinami's election activities, were addressed to the group's members, but in November 1983 neither Ezoe nor Recruit belonged to the group, so the five-million-yen donation could not have been provided in response to such a written request for funds. Three years later, at the time of the general elections of 1986, Recruit did respond to such a request and remitted funds into the designated account, but on that occasion the contribution was merely two hundred thousand yen. A comparison of the two amounts suffices to rule out that the five million yen provided in November 1983 was a donation in response to a request for election support, and in fact these circumstances were objectively acknowledged.

It is clear, based on the evidence, that the five-million-yen donation made to Fujinami in the form of a check was not provided on a one-time basis to support his election activities, but was one of the political donations regularly rendered to him by Recruit.

On this point too, the views expressed in the two court rulings differed. The Mikami ruling was this:

> *Although, as the prosecution points out, a great number of deposits were made into the account in question that are thought to be funds to support campaigning activities in timing with elections, it appears that political contributions were also regularly made into the account by specific companies. It is therefore impossible to affirm that the account was used largely to receive election campaign funds.*

The Yamamuro ruling, by contrast, attempted, by forced logic if necessary, to admit the contention made by the prosecution. Following are excerpts:

The provision of the check in November 1983 took place immediately before the general elections of December 18th.

Judging also from the fact that November 28th would be too early for a "year-end gift" [whereas donations were made around December 19th in 1984, around December 5th in 1985, and around December 3rd in 1987], it is reasonable to see the provision of the check in November 1983 as having been made in preparation for the general elections.

In contrast to provisions of checks between June and mid-July in 1985 [on June 26th], 1986 [on June 9th], 1987 [on July 16th] and 1988 [on June 17th and 22nd], in 1984 the provision was carried out around August 10th, notably later than in other years. This discrepancy can be reasonably understood by the fact that before the summer of 1984 no regular donations were made and, as the defendant [Ezoe] stated during the investigation phase, just prior to providing the check in August of that year, he offered to make regular donations to Fujinami; the check provided around August 10th can be seen as the first such donation, with subsequent provisions rendered on a regular basis between June and mid-July to meet expenses during the summer season.

The foremost problem is the fact that during the interrogations, no questions about the check of November 1983 were posed to anyone connected not just with Ezoe but with Fujinami either.

The Yamamuro ruling also points this out in the following manner:

It would seem only natural to look further into the dissimilarity between the purport of the November donation and the purport of the donations made after August 1984. Had that been done, it would be difficult to view as reasonable what Prosecutor Munakata testified as to why he did not seek explanation from the defendant [Ezoe], and substantial doubt would remain as to whether at the time of their investigation the prosecutors were aware of the fact that a check had been provided in November 1983.

The Mikami ruling expresses nearly the same view:

If an understanding were to be achieved of the details of the provision of the check from November 1983, it would seem only natural for explanations concerning this point to have been sought from the defendant's [Fujinami's] secretaries, Tokuda and Mizutani, and from Ono at Recruit, who was in charge of the paperwork for the funding provided to the defendant. But as we have seen earlier, no such interrogations were conducted and Prosecutor Munakata himself has given no logical explanation for his failure to seek elaboration on this point from Ezoe; in light of which, it is impossible to erase doubts that at the time of their investigation the prosecutors may not have been aware of the fact of the provision of that check in November 1983.

An unbiased look at how this investigation was conducted would suggest that the interrogating prosecutor questioned Ezoe on the premise that the regular donations had commenced in August 1984, and the natural conclusion to be drawn from this is that he drew up a written statement to match his scenario.

The cited rulings notwithstanding, when it came to evaluating Ezoe's testimony and written statements the two judges expressed polar opposite views. The Mikami ruling, in response to how the investigation had been conducted, opined:

The various statements made by Ezoe and other parties concerned during the investigation phase relating to the period when Recruit began providing political donations absolutely cannot be taken at face value.

The judge then proceeded to come to an extremely sensible conclusion:

In reference to the various statements contending that regular dona-
tions by Recruit to the defendant [Fujinami] began before August
1984, given that a check was in fact provided in November 1983 and
that it cannot be established that the purport of said check was to
serve as political funding on a one-time basis, the credibility of such
statements cannot be denied.

Contrastingly, the Yamamuro ruling holds steadfastly to Ezoe's statements as drawn up by the prosecutor:

In reference to the charge that the defendant [Ezoe] passed bribes
to Fujinami, the defendant underwent interrogation in the form of
a voluntary investigation during his post-indictment detention,
and he participated in those interrogations while meeting with his
defense counsel for long hours almost every day; therefore, given
the circumstances of those interrogations, we can find no cause to
doubt their voluntary nature. Also, regarding the statements made
by the defendant concerning his having made regular donations to
Fujinami after August 1984, it can be concluded that he repeatedly
consulted with his defense counsel, personally mulled over mat-
ters over the course of several days, and then acquiesced to pre-
pared written statements the content of which he found to be to his
satisfaction.

Here, the judge demonstrates a stance in which he pays little heed to the fact that the prosecutors undertook their interrogations totally ignoring the donation made in November 1983 and seeking to accord maximum importance to the content of the written statements.

Connection with the Personnel Chiefs' Meeting

The Mikami ruling had this to say about the "agreement" reached at
the meeting of personnel department heads at the various government
agencies:

> *It has never been demonstrated that when Nakamura reported to
> Fujinami, Fujinami gave instructions to take specific steps to pre-
> vent early recruitment by the government agencies. There is also no
> evidence whatsoever indicating that the agreement reached at the
> meeting of personnel chiefs came as a result of any asking by Ezoe of
> Fujinami or any pressure applied by Recruit.*

The Yamamuro ruling, on the other hand, says that at the time Ezoe met
with Fujinami, it was not assured that the personnel chiefs would agree to
adhere to the gentlemen's agreement. It says the possibility that there was
no connection between Ezoe's actions and the agreement cannot be ruled
out. And it says that since the situation was such that if moves to bring
the date forward were to fail, the early recruitment problem was projected
to remain unresolved, and it is not unreasonable for Ezoe to have asked
Fujinami to take steps to prevent early recruitment. In other words, the
Yamamuro ruling says that at the time of Ezoe's visit to Fujinami, because
it was not certain that an agreement would be reached, it is not unreasonable to think that the topic came up.

Lastly, the two rulings touch upon the intent of, and awareness surrounding, the share transfers.

The Mikami ruling:

> *According to the prosecution's contentions, the specific step alleg-
> edly taken by the defendant [Fujinami] to prevent early recruitment
> by the government agencies was his getting the agreement reached at
> the meeting of personnel chiefs. However, the agreement reached at
> the meeting in 1984 was realized not through any initiatives taken*

by the defendant, but rather came about in the wake of negotiations between the National Personnel Authority and the Nikkeiren and other economic organizations, when, in lieu of bringing forward the date for announcing the results of the civil service exam, it was agreed to cooperate in hiring of public servants by honoring the gentlemen's agreement of the private sector. The similar agreement reached at the personnel chiefs' meeting of 1985 too was merely a follow-up to the agreement of the previous year and did not need any initiatives to be taken by the defendant. Also, there is no reason to think that Recruit, which had been gathering information relating to the agreement reached at the meeting of 1984, got the agreement reached at the meeting through efforts of the defendant; nor is there reason to believe that the defendant was thanked by Recruit for having arranged the agreement at the meeting.

Then again:

In relation to the transfer of Recruit Cosmos shares, the court acknowledges that direct telephone contact was made from Ezoe to the defendant, but from Ezoe's testimony the court finds nothing at all to suggest that in Ezoe's explanation at the time there was anything indicating, either explicitly or implicitly, that the sale of shares was an expression of gratitude for the foregoing favors.

The Yamamuro ruling, however, reads as follows:

Insofar as the defendant [Ezoe] is concerned, even without clearly indicating the intent of a reward pertaining to the favors, it would suffice for Fujinami to grasp that intent intuitively. Also, if the defendant were to do anything blatantly indicating its intent as bribery, that would conceivably make the recipient, a politician, wary of engaging in such an indiscreet act. Therefore, it is not unreasonable that the defendant, instead of indicating that the shares were a reward for doing the favors requested by him, sold the shares with their purport left implicit.

Written Statements and Video Recording of Interrogations

In Japan, in cases like bribery, where the issue is whether something was asked for and whether money or other good was given as reward for fulfilling the request, the issue always revolves around what is stated during the interrogations and what is recorded in written statements. The reason is that normally no records of conversations are kept—all the more so when the sentiment is to thank the receiving party—and the only means of knowing what transpired is from the statements made by the person under investigation.

Inherently, statements written up by prosecutors or police officers are supposed to record what the interrogated party said precisely, and must be signed by that party. The reality, however, is often altogether otherwise.

It frequently happens that things a party never said get recorded as having been said, or statements get prepared and signed claiming that events that never occurred did indeed take place. Such things often occur not only in cases involving bribery or election violations, but even in cases involving murder or robbery.

Many people likely believe that in cases like murder, where a conviction could result in the death penalty, nobody would ever sign his or her name to a statement that testifies to something that in fact he or she did not do. "*I* would never sign, *never*," they say. The Yamamuro ruling suggests something similar: "No matter how much a prosecutor might want the accused to sign a statement in line with what he had in mind, it is difficult to conceive that he would engage in such blatant tactics to have his way."

The reality, however, is that such things actually do occur, and this case is no exception. Nearly all the cases purported to have involved false charges were cases in which convictions were won based on the defendant's confession.

I myself have been involved in the defense of defendants for whom the prosecutors sought the death penalty. Not just the defendant being charged, but virtually all the people said to have been accomplices, signed statements saying they did something they actually did not do.

An example is the case involving an explosion at a post office on the basement floor of the Nippon Oil Corporation in the Nishi-Shimbashi area of Tokyo in October 1971. A postal employee had taken receipt of two small parcels, and when he tossed them into the appropriate pouch, they exploded, causing him injury.

The employee testified that the two items had been brought by two women in office attire. A series of arrests and indictments were made in the case, charging the two women as well as the alleged ringleader and various individuals who were said to have transported the parcels.

As put together by the investigating team, the story up to the time the parcels were handed over at the post office reads as follows:

E, a mechanic working at a car repair shop in Ogikubo, was asked by the ringleader, M, to collect two parcels in storage, then come to pick up M and a woman, Y, nearby and take them to Shinjuku Chuo Park. At the park they met up with R, who was waiting for them in another car. M and Y got into E's car, M in the passenger seat and Y in the rear seat. R then drove to Shimbashi, discharging his passengers fifty meters from the Nippon Oil building. At that point Y met up with N, another woman, who had been waiting for her, and the two went to the post office with the two parcels. After posting the parcels, N met up with S, who was waiting near Shimbashi Station, and S drove N to Matsudo, in Chiba Prefecture.

The statement is extremely detailed concerning the circumstances as to how the parcel relay took place, including not only R's involvement but also that of M, the alleged ringleader, and the other drivers E and S. For example, R's statement given to police investigators records a long list of events that could have been elaborated upon only by the person who had actually experienced them. To illustrate: "*I went to the specified park at*

9:40, ten minutes later than the designated time of 9:30. E was already there, and M and Y were waiting behind E's car, as if they were hiding." Then again: "Y, in the rear seat, was holding the paper bags on her lap, her hands pressing down on them as though they were very important." And as if that weren't enough, the statement also records in minute detail the plotting that took place two days before the actual relay. Later, however, it was determined that the events recorded in these statements were total fabrications, and eventually the Metropolitan Police Department that prepared the statements testified that the statements contained lies. For at the precise time the parcels exploded in the post office, R, who allegedly drove M and Y to Shimbashi, was in fact taking the written test for his driver's license in Fuchu. What this means is that E's relaying his passengers to R in Shinjuku, where R continued the relay to S at Shimbashi, and M and Y's having gone from Ogikubo to Shimbashi were all fabrications.

Needless to say, during interrogations, it was absolutely impossible for the accused individuals, being in detention, to meet or to have any contact with one other. Why, in spite of that, were statements prepared, simultaneously, to fit the investigators' scenario, not just in reference to R but to M, E, and S as well? What on earth could have been their reason?

The only persons who could have had mutual contact with the accused and could have prepared statements consistent with one another were the investigators—the interrogating police officers and prosecutors. It is inconceivable that anyone else was involved. They forced the accused to go along with the scenario they concocted and made them sign the statements that had been drawn up to support that scenario. In Japan, the punishment for violating the penal code controlling explosive substances, that is, for using an explosive substance, is death or life imprisonment. Even though they didn't commit the crime, and in spite of the heavy punishment that might have awaited them, the accused nevertheless agreed to affix their signatures to false statements. One can imagine how in cases like bribery, where the accused are assured that by signing they will quickly be released on bail or be given a suspended sentence, that the accused will give in and sign. Humans give in to such temptations easily.

In the case of the Recruit trial, the verdicts handed down turned on the credibility of such written statements, which would seem certified by the person who attested to details. But as we see from the example just cited, it is altogether easy for investigators to make up some spurious scenario and work it up into a written statement.

Because of this inherent risk surrounding written statements, inevitably questions arise in court as to the credibility of what is recorded in statements. Were the statements drawn up with the accused's free will? Did the accused sign statements that record precisely what he had said? Legally speaking, were the statements and their signing voluntary in nature?

To answer such questions, questioning goes on in court for hours concerning the voluntariness and credibility of statements. Both the accused and the interrogating officers undergo examination about how the interrogations were conducted. The Recruit case was no exception. Without exaggeration, it can be said that the lion's share of the more than three hundred court sessions was spent dealing with these issues.

Despite the long hours a court may spend deliberating these matters, ultimately there is the tendency of the court to find the contents of the written statements more believable than the oral testimony given in the courtroom by the party concerned. This prejudice can be said to be what's wrong with the criminal trial system in Japan today.

Why do courts favor written statements over oral testimony? The answer may seem to beg the question, but the reason is, they always have. This has been their practice overwhelmingly, and that is why investigators will go to any lengths to prepare such statements. This vicious circle gives rise to what ails the judicial system. And it is the nation's judges—the agents of the court—who trust statements drawn up by police officers and investigators behind closed doors rather than the content of testimony given before their eyes. This perpetuates this situation.

What methods might be used to cure this ailment?

Since the end of the Second World War, various debates have taken place concerning this matter. Indeed, one might say the topic has been debated exhaustively. For their part, the investigators profess that they cannot extract the truth from the accused unless they are behind closed doors. Hence, the belief that confession is the highest form of proof. In modern times, however, criminal trials are conducted by establishing facts through the accumulation of objective and circumstantial evidence, without relying on confessions. Outside Japan, measures of various sorts have been taken in light of the risks surrounding so-called confessions.

In the United States, the Supreme Court established what is known as the Miranda Rule. It is based on the Fifth Amendment to the Constitution, which states: "No person . . . shall be compelled in any criminal case to be a witness against himself, nor be deprived of life, liberty, or property, without due process of law." The first part of the cited passage is referred to as the "Right against Self-Incrimination."

The Miranda Rule reads, in part, as follows:

> . . . *the prosecution may not use statements, whether exculpatory or inculpatory, stemming from custodial interrogation of the defendant unless it demonstrates the use of procedural safeguards effective to secure the privilege against self-incrimination. By custodial interrogation, we mean questioning initiated by law enforcement officers after a person has been taken into custody or otherwise deprived of his freedom of action in any significant way. As for the procedural safeguards to be employed, unless other fully effective means are devised to inform accused persons of their right of silence and to assure a continuous opportunity to exercise it, the following measures are required. Prior to any questioning, the person must be warned that he has a right to remain silent, that any statement he does make may be used as evidence against him, and that he has a right to the presence of an attorney, either retained or appointed. The defendant may waive effectuation of these rights, provided the waiver is made voluntarily, knowingly and intelligently. If, however, he indicates in any manner and at any stage of the process that he wishes to consult with an attorney before speaking there can be no questioning. Likewise, if the individual is alone and*

indicates in any manner that he does not wish to be interrogated, the police may not question him. The mere fact that he may have answered some questions or volunteered some statements on his own does not deprive him of the right to refrain from answering any further inquiries until he has consulted with an attorney and thereafter consents to be questioned. —Miranda v. Arizona, 384 U.S. 436 (1966)

At the end of each episode of the TV series *Columbo*, after Columbo has finally caught his culprit and is about to arrest him, the card he pulls out of his pocket and begins reading is none other than this "Miranda warning." In a nutshell, this is a statement to the person about to be arrested that he has, among other rights, the right to have an attorney present when he is interrogated; and in the event that, upon being notified of that right, the person willingly chooses to waive that right, then any statements prepared without an attorney present cannot, barring substantiation by the prosecuting side, be used as evidence of guilt.

How this warning is currently carried out in the United States is a matter of great interest. But in Japan too, finally, testing has recently gotten underway toward making interrogations and the circumstances under which they are conducted visible by means of audio and/or video recording. Bringing open visibility to interrogations can be achieved in various ways, to varying degrees of effectiveness. Needless to say, there is a world of difference when an attorney is present or when the interrogation proceedings are actually recorded on tape or video.

As to the right to have a lawyer present during an interrogation, this is something the Japanese Ministry of Justice and the National Police Agency absolutely refuse to allow. At the very most, they show a willingness to permit partial recording. But with partial recording, audio or video, there is an extremely high risk that this could actually be used to cover up unlawful interrogation methods. Past cases of convictions that were ultimately shown to have been built on false charges demonstrate this risk all too well.

It is hoped that under the new administration a legal framework will be put into place for conducting full recording of all phases of all interrogations, as current calls now demand. Even if such a framework is established, however, problems are likely to remain.

The only fundamental solution would seem to be refusal to recognize the value, as evidence, of any statement prepared without an attorney present.

Shozaburo Ishida. Born in 1946. Graduated from Chuo University, Faculty of Law, passed the bar exam, 1969. Entered the Legal Training and Research Institute of Japan, 1971. Became an Attorney at Law registered with the Dai-ni Tokyo Bar Association, 1973. Established Sengoku & Ishida Law Office, 1983, reorganized as Ishida & Chinzei Law Office, 2007.

Has served as chairman of the Criminal Defense Committee and deputy chairman of the Permanent Members Council of the Dai-ni Tokyo Bar Association, and as vice chairman of the Criminal Defense Center of the Japan Federation of Bar Associations.

III

RE THE LAY JUDGE SYSTEM AND PROPOSALS FOR REFORM

Hiromasa Ezoe

Doubts and Suggestions

The Selection Pool

Under the judicial system now in place, lay judges are drawn from the pool of the entire nation's eligible voters, which is to say, all Japanese citizens age twenty and above. Personally, I wonder if it is prudent to include *all* voters within this pool.

In my opinion, young people just above twenty years of age still do not have a strong understanding of the world around them. The college enrollment rate in Japan is roughly fifty percent, which means that half of all citizens around the age of twenty are students—people who have no experience in the real world making a living, working for a company. Young people also have a low voting rate in national elections, a fact that reflects their low level of interest in society.

Surely, someone on trial would wonder whether anyone so young and inexperienced would be capable of passing proper judgment.

The current system poses problems for people who are selected to serve as lay judges as well.

Citizens chosen to be candidates to serve as lay judges are given the option of declining if they are above the age of seventy or if they have a "compelling" reason. The distinction between a compelling reason and a non-compelling reason is unclear, however. In the case of someone with a job, for example, being chosen to serve as a lay judge could create compelling issues.

Suppose this person worked at a bank as a loan officer or a loan inspector. If he or she were to be absent for a period of time, loan operations would come to a halt. As a consequence, a company that had been counting on securing a loan could conceivably go under. Or suppose an experienced engineer in charge of blast furnace or rolling operations at a steel mill were selected as a lay judge, the entire time he was in court would create a situation where concerns over the firm's product quality were raised.

For the past twenty-five years I have been going to the same barbershop once a month. The shop is owned and operated by one man, working alone—a circumstance that is not unusual in Japan: fishmongers, greengrocers, small restaurants, etc. are similar. If such individuals were selected to serve as lay judges, they would be unable to operate their business and suffer a decline in sales. Conversely, their customers would find the need to go elsewhere.

When I was young, I had the experience of planting rice. The time best suited to planting rice is only about one week long, varying from year to year depending on the weather. If the planting does not get done during that one week, the harvest could suffer. If a rice farmer is called to serve duty as a lay judge at this critical time, how will he be compensated for any decrease in his harvest? Or what about those employed in the fishing industry, where all boats take to the seas the date the fishing season opens? If a ship's captain were called to serve in court, he would be unable to send out his ship. Obviously he stands to suffer a loss of income.

In view of situations like these, rather than selecting lay judges at random, I think there would be less of a burden on society if lay judges were chosen from among citizens who wish to perform a service to society and who have the time to spare. It would be appropriate, for example, to select lay judges from among people who serve as family court arbitrators, people who are retired or have no work obligations, or housewives who have completed child-rearing.

Such citizens, it seems to me, would have life experience as well, and would be preferred by individuals on trial to lay judges selected at random.

Legal Language

The language employed in Japan's legal codes is quite difficult, creating obstacles to a correct understanding of the nation's laws for the average citizen.

To illustrate, Article 38 of the Criminal Code, which deals with "intent," reads as follows:

> *(1) An act performed without the intent to commit a crime is not punishable; provided, however, that the same shall not apply in cases where otherwise specially provided for by law.*
>
> *(2) When a person who commits a crime is not, at the time of its commission, aware of the facts constituting a greater crime, the person shall not be punished for the greater crime.*
>
> *(3) Lacking knowledge of law shall not be deemed lacking the intention to commit a crime; provided, however, that punishment may be reduced in light of the circumstance.*

Given these guidelines, how can anyone judge whether a given act was or was not performed with "intent"?

Or consider Article 37 of the same code as concerns "averting present danger":

> *(1) An act unavoidably performed to avert a present danger to the life, body, liberty or property of oneself or any other person is not punishable only when the harm produced by such act does not exceed the harm to be averted; provided, however, that an act causing excessive harm may lead to the punishment being reduced or may exculpate the offender in light of the circumstances.*

(2) The preceding paragraph does not apply to a person under special professional obligation.

A lay judge would surely be at a loss as to how specifically to interpret what this means.

Such difficulty can be seen no less in the general provisions of the "Lay Judge Act." Article 1 states that "the Act serves to set down special provisions, along with other necessary matters, to the Court Act (Act No. 59) and the Code of Criminal Procedure (Act No. 131) relating to criminal trials in which lay judges participate, in light of the fact that the involvement of lay judges selected from among the nation's citizens, together with court judges, in criminal legal procedures will contribute to enhancing citizens' understanding of, and trust in, the judicial system."

This is one sentence that comprises the entire article, and it is not unusual in that regard. Subsequent articles are in almost all instances one very long sentence as well. This arcane language is evidenced in Japan's six legal codes. It may be comprehensible to members of the bar, but it would seem beyond the understanding of the average citizen. How then can they be expected to interpret the law?

If average citizens are to serve effectively as lay judges, and if the system is to function effectively, rewriting the nation's laws so that they can be understood is necessary.

Appropriate Cases for Trial by Lay Judges

Specifying criminal cases—especially those involving homicide, robbery, and the like—as cases to be tried by lay judges seems to me highly questionable. Personally, I think the lay judge system would better prove its worth when applied to civil court cases such as divorce or inheritance disputes.

Despite an increasing number of divorces in Japan in recent years, the nation's laws pertaining to divorce are not as clear as they are in other countries. Disputes over inheritances also seem to be on the rise, but when cases involving distribution of property and the like go to court, decisions are made by judges who live in a world apart from the average person. It would seem that individuals involved in such cases would more readily accept judgments passed down from the perspective of citizens with broader life experience.

Take, for example, my own situation. My wife, who became a religious fanatic, filed for a divorce, and this took us to court over how to divide up our assets. When I requested that our daughters appear as witnesses—the elder worked for a company for six years and is now at home raising a family, and the younger lives in Italy, where she paints and works in the theater—the court rejected both requests. The judges appeared not to recognize that divorce cases involve more than just numerical issues concerning property; they are also accompanied by mental anguish for both parties.

After making this point in the Japanese edition of this book, I received this letter from an attorney:

> In reference to your suggestion that lay judges serve in civil court cases, since 2004 a system has been introduced in which one male and one female sit in on trials where the divorce is the point of dispute. The system is not adopted in criminal trials. The men and women selected to serve are chosen from people with many years' experience as mediators in family court cases, and they deliberate in divorce cases together with the judge. Their participation is quite significant, I think, because they ask questions from a perspective different from that of a judge. I can therefore well understand the point of your suggestion.

When the lay judge system comes up for review, I hope this suggestion will be given serious thought.

I have another reason for believing that the lay judge system is suited to civil rather than criminal cases.

An acquaintance, a former first associate judge, had written the judgment that imposed the death penalty on a particular defendant. This so weighed on him that he later quit the bench and became a lawyer—something he might not have been able to do had he waited until near retirement age. He was still young enough to make a fresh start, although to this very day, he has said, he regretted having written that judgment.

In a similar instance, Megumi Yamamuro, the presiding judge who handed down the verdict in my own trial, told me one reason he had stepped down from the bench midway through his appointment was because of the death sentence he handed down in the Aum Shinrikyo case, in which members of the religious cult were convicted of murdering a lawyer and his family in 1989.

These are the sentiments of people who have actually handed down a death sentence—judges who by their profession knew full well that there might be times when they would have to. How much greater the mental burden must be for the average citizen in such a situation.

Another problem is that when lay judges have to pass judgment on serious crimes such as homicide, in order to identify the cause of death they will be required to view, if not the crime site itself, the site on video or in photographs. This is not as simple as it would seem; many a person is not capable of doing this.

For example, a physician acquaintance reported seeing young doctors, many of them male, become incontinent, vomit, or faint when observing surgery. Shozaburo Ishida, one of my defense attorneys, told me about a police officer who fainted during an autopsy. If this happens to professionals in the field, imagine the distress average citizens would undergo.

And in fact, in the very first trial adopting the lay judge system, the media reported that when the lay judges looked away from disturbing photos or video images, the prosecution exhorted them to look squarely at what was being shown to them.

If the lay judge system is to continue to be used in criminal cases, I propose that the cases be limited to nonviolent crimes—for example, theft, gropings, etc. Elsewise, confine the system to civil cases. Why it was ever decided to limit the system to major crimes like homicide and robbery is beyond comprehension.

Safety of Lay Judges

The newly introduced system needs also to address the safety of the lay judges.

Article 3 of the Lay Judge Act sets down the following stipulation:

> *In reference to the cases named in the various Clauses of the preceding Article, in the event that the district court determines that, because of actions by the defendant, or claims made by an organization of which the defendant is a member, or words or actions by other members of such organization, or any actual harm or warning of harm to a lay judge candidate or lay judge, or other circumstances, there is fear that harm may come to the life, body or property of a lay judge candidate, lay judge, one who was formerly a lay judge, a family relation of same or anyone in a corresponding position, or that the situation makes it difficult to secure the appearance in court of such individual, or a lay judge cannot carry out his duties and selecting an alternate lay judge is difficult, then by request of the prosecution, the defendant or the defense attorney, or by professional prerogative, a decision must be rendered for the case to be handled by a panel of court judges.*

As to trials not applicable to the lay judge system, however, the situation is ambiguous. In a trial dealing with a crime committed by a member of a syndicate, for example, there is a possibility of a threat to the lay judge. Let me explain by this example:

In the Yoshiwara, Kabukicho, and Kinshicho areas of Tokyo, as well as Horinouchi in Kawasaki, Fukuhara in Kobe, and Nakasu in Fukuoka, there are red-light districts. After enactment of the Anti-Prostitution Act in 1956, prostitution technically became an unlawful act, yet today it is carried out in the open, the reason generally assumed by the public to be that this business is run by the Japanese mafia.

Suppose a murder-robbery were to occur at such a location and someone connected to a syndicate were caught and put on trial before lay judges.

Surely the possibility exists that lay judges and members of their families would be harassed or threatened.

When I was president of Recruit Cosmos, a dog's corpse was left on the doorstep of my home in Zushi by someone opposed to the company's construction of a condominium. Although I didn't think any direct harm would come to me personally, I felt great unease about the safety of my daughter who was in kindergarten at the time.

But if something like this were to occur in connection with a case being tried by lay judges, selected citizens would think twice about serving, and alternates kept in reserve would hesitate as well. Under such circumstances, I imagine that if any major incident did occur, people would shy away from serving as lay judges even if they were appointed.

According to a National Police Agency official, the Criminal Investigation Bureau maintains files on organized crime groups nationwide, and as of the end of 2004 such groups had a total of 44,000 full-fledged members—87,000 when quasi-members were included. If smaller criminal organizations for which the police have no data were added in, the total number would likely more than double.

All of this is brought up to point to the need of the judicial system to ensure the personal safety of lay judges.

Obligation of Lay Judges to Maintain Secrecy

Lay judges are forbidden to reveal, at any time in their lives, the content of their deliberations in the trial in which they were involved. If they do reveal such information, they are liable to criminal penalty. This seems like unduly harsh punishment.

Is it not human nature to be overcome by the urge to tell others about a case you have been involved in, especially if it is a violent crime?

A lay judge, who would be beholden to his fellow workers for the inconvenience his absence may have caused them, might let something slip while having drinks with them. Is that so terrible a wrongdoing?

For example, when you are involved in a case that attracts public attention, journalists and reporters will not leave you alone until you blurt something out. I know that from experience. Once, when I was living in Zushi, it was reported in the press that I, along with a group of people, had gone to Las Vegas to gamble. The next day I was besieged by reporters from the weekly magazines who pressed me for comments as I tried to walk the fifteen minutes to the train station. I was bursting to tell them I hadn't gone to Las Vegas to gamble but to see Diana Ross and the Supremes, en route to New York, where I had business. I also wanted to tell them that even if I *had* gone to Las Vegas to gamble, there was nothing wrong in that. I stifled the urge, however, and merely requested that they go through the public relations office at Recruit. After that I said nothing.

I think only those who have actually had experience with the media would understand what I'm talking about, but the methods used by members of the media to get a story are numerous and varied. The average person who is not accustomed to such things would likely, in some instances, give in to the ploys used by members of the media and end up saying something they might regret.

A former judge who is an acquaintance told me that when a judge is presiding over a trial in a major case, the judges' wives often talk about the case together at their government lodgings.

Lay Judge Trials in the High Courts

Following the close of the first trial using the lay judge system in August 2009, a legal expert interviewed on television indicated that the punishment meted out in the case had been a bit too heavy. Shozaburo Ishida, my attorney in the Recruit trial, concurred; professional judges would have handed down a lighter sentence.

Few if any lay judges have a proper understanding of what crimes warrant what punishments. With a murder case, I think the measure set by the average citizen would likely be harsher than the penalty handed down by a professional judge. With a jury system, the jury members render a decision only as to guilt or innocence; the punishment is decided by the judge. To my thinking, it would be better if court judges were to decide on punishments under the lay judge system as well.

In Japan, judicial process allows for a defendant, if dissatisfied with the ruling handed down in a district court, to appeal to a higher court. The lay judge system, however, is applicable only to cases heard in the district courts.

If a heavy punishment is handed down by lay judges in a district court trial, the defendant is likely to appeal. On the other hand, if the punishment is light, the prosecution is likely to appeal. Either way, by appealing the initial decision, the case will revert to a conventional trial in which no lay judges participate. What value then is there in the trial by lay judges?

In Japan, the conviction rate in criminal trials is close to 99.9 percent. As to how this phenomenal figure is achievable, *Sentaku*, an independent monthly information magazine, had this to say in its issue of September 2008:

> *When the prosecution appeals [a ruling handed down by the district court], in eight out of ten cases the decision is overturned in the high court in the prosecution's favor. In other words, the conviction rate in Japan must be said to be "infinitely close to 100 percent."*
>
> *Even the meager 0.1 percent of cases in which a ruling of not guilty is initially handed down end up getting overturned in the prosecution's favor, ultimately leading to the abnormality of an "infallible" criminal justice system, invariably aligned to the prosecution's claims, centered on the Tokyo High Court.*

In the Recruit trial also, Masao Tatsumi was initially pronounced innocent in the district court, only subsequently to be found guilty, based on virtually the identical evidence, by the high court. Former Chief Cabinet Secretary Fujinami, too, was declared innocent in the district court but, after that decision was slammed by the media, was ruled guilty in the high court, again based on nearly the same evidence. The media reported that the prosecution had won a "thin-ice victory."

As of this writing, in all trials in which the lay judge system has been applied, the defendant has admitted his guilt. I wonder whether, if the system is introduced only into district court trials, the current situation surrounding such trials—in which innocent people can be falsely charged, as in the "Ashikaga case" (about which, more later)—will really change. It seems to me like "grafting bamboo to a tree"—that is, I just don't see the logic to it.

If the newly launched lay judge system is to be maintained, it should be applied at least in high court trials, and perhaps in the Supreme Court, too.

Questioning by Victims

In December 2008, Japan adopted a system under which victims can participate in the trial of the alleged perpetrator of the crime. In some major cases of this kind, the victim (or a proxy) has been able to question the defendant. Here again, I have reservations about this system.

First, the defendant has not been proven to be the actual perpetrator. The victim, however, assumes from the outset that the defendant is in fact the person who committed the crime against him. Obviously, the defendant, if he is not the perpetrator, will state in court that he has not committed the crime he is accused of. In such instances, one can imagine that the emotions of the victim, convinced that the defendant is the culprit, will take over. "Why do you lie?" the victim might scream to the defendant. "Admit what you've done and apologize!" The defendant refuses to back down, and continues to proclaim his innocence. "Why should I apologize for something I haven't done?" At that point the defendant and the victim wage a fierce battle of words. Attempts by the presiding judge or lay judges to intervene prove futile, and the proceedings fly out of control. This is not a desired scenario, and yet it is not unlikely.

Inherently, a criminal trial is a venue for probing whether or not the accused is the actual perpetrator of the crime. In order to arrive at a fair and level-headed judgment, it seems preferable that the trial not be a place where the victim can make a display of his emotions. My hope is that questioning by victims of crime will be abolished when the system is slated to come up for review in 2012.

Length of Court Proceedings

The reason my interrogations and trial dragged on to such great length is because I denied the charges against me.

In cases dealing with violent crime—murder-robbery, for example—trials by professional judges take a minimum of one year. But the "Shibushi case" (about this, more later), a relatively simple case involving election fraud in a small city in Kagoshima Prefecture in 2003, went on for more than a year.

When the defendant denies the charges against him, in order to hand down a fair ruling the court finds it necessary to summon and obtain testimony from witnesses, close relatives, neighbors, etc.

In the Ashikaga case mentioned earlier, seventeen years passed between the time of the defendant Toshikazu Sugaya's arrest and conviction and the court's ultimately finding him innocent. At the time this turn of events was reported on television, some fifteen audio tapes of his interrogations were made public. Listening to all of them would alone require a great deal of time. If judges and lay judges were properly to listen to all the tapes and then commence their deliberations, more than a few days would be necessary. As envisioned, the lay judge system, however, expects that roughly seventy percent of all cases will be completed within three days, about ninety percent within five days. But since interrogations generally require a period of about twenty days, in order to arrive at the truth in all cases, would it not be necessary that there be a wider time span allocated to court proceedings—anywhere from three days to a month?

Furthermore, since the accused can be detained for seventy-two hours between the time of his arrest and his indictment, plus twenty days, the prosecution has ample time to conduct its interrogations. Given the length of those interrogations, in consideration of the time needed by the lay judges to read the statements in the case, stipulating three to five days for the trial seems very much out of balance. Should a more lengthy trial be warranted, then a more lengthy trial should be held. If a lay judge cannot fulfill his role for a trial lasting ten days or more, then he could be relieved of his duties.

Proposals for Reforming the Justice System

Introduction of a Jury System

In the United States, a jury system modeled on England's has been in use ever since the nation was founded. The American justice system varies in specifics from state to state, but the jury system has remained in use for over two centuries, with improvements effected from time to time as deemed necessary.

I believe that if the American jury system were introduced into Japan, with modifications to make it suit Japanese society, it would be a new justice system that the Japanese people would readily find agreeable.

In the postwar years Japan scored its rapid growth while paying patent fees to the United States in areas like industrial products and textiles. For a time Japan even ranked No.1, the oil-producing nations aside, in per capita GDP. Whenever an expert in American affairs proclaims, "This is how they do it in America," many Japanese nod in quiet assent. In Japan, thinking up totally unique notions is a very difficult process. Then, of course, just getting the people to go along with it requires tremendous time and effort.

Instead of introducing a lay judge system unique to Japan and gradually revising it, all would go more smoothly if the country adopted the jury system used in the United States and modified its purposes to suit Japan.

Full Video Recording of Interrogations and Notification of Rights

In theory, the job of a prosecutor is to interrogate a suspect to learn whether he is innocent or guilty; in reality, however, the mission of the prosecution is to win a guilty verdict against the accused. This is clear from the fact that, as noted earlier, in Japan the conviction rate in criminal cases is close to 99.9 percent.

During my interrogations in the Recruit affair, against my will I signed statements that were untrue based on promises by the prosecutors that if I signed I would get a suspended sentence or get out on bail quickly. Out of fear, I was compelled to sign statements drawn up by the prosecution relating to things I had *not* said. Threats were made to the effect that if I did not sign, I would remain in detention for as long as it took and I would suffer for it. There were also a number of instances in which the prosecutors drew up statements by witnesses containing things that were not true, but that they were forced to sign. (I have detailed these instances at length in *Where Is the Justice?: Media Attacks, Prosecutorial Abuse, and My 13 Years in Japanese Court*, published a year ago.)

At my trial, the prosecutors in their opening remarks stated that I had visited Chief Cabinet Secretary Fujinami to ask him to do something about the schedule of the civil service exam, and that Hisao Tanaka, senior managing director at Recruit, and others had paid a similar visit the following year. These remarks were based on Tanaka's statement, which was coerced. Tanaka had been summoned to the National Police Agency more than fifty times and had been threatened with arrest if he did not sign the statements investigators had prepared. He said he had no alternative but to sign.

Toshikazu Sugaya, the person accused in the Ashikaga murder case mentioned above, has said that on the first day of his interrogations, he had been threatened and forced to sign a written statement of confession. During his trial, he said, he had been too scared to tell the truth because the interrogating police officers were in the courtroom.

In my case, I had already been harshly dealt with during my voluntary interrogations, so when I was subjected to harsh interrogations again after my arrest, I no longer felt the same fear. But it is not difficult to imagine how someone who gets arrested out of the blue and is put through severe questioning can break down and sign a statement drawn up by the prosecutor, however false it may be.

At his press conference following his release, Sugaya expressed his anger openly, demanding apologies from the police officers and prosecutors who had interrogated him. Subsequently, on behalf of those officers and prosecutors, Tochigi Prefectural Police Chief Shoichiro Ishikawa and Utsunomiya Chief Public Prosecutor Hideo Makuta extended their apologies to Sugaya. No amount of apologizing can bring back the time he lost in prison, however.

The Ashikaga case is by no means unique: coercive interrogations appear to have been carried out in many other cases as well. To avoid such forced confessions as well as to enable lay judges to render more accurate judgments during trials, the introduction of full video recording of all interrogations is necessary.

Today, prosecutors undertake partial recording, on video and audio tape, of their interrogation procedures. Such recording is *not* complete—it is but a stance apparently taken in order to shorten the time involved. But this policy is extremely disadvantageous to the accused. Because the prosecution can choose to record on video only those parts that work to its advantage, this actually increases the likelihood of statements that disadvantage the arrested.

Assume, for example, that the prosecutor draws up a statement suiting his own purposes, drives the accused into a corner by telling him that if he signs the statement he will be released on bail early but if he chooses not to sign he will remain in detention, and the accused gives in to that threat and signs. The result is a signature obtained as a result of behind-the-scenes plea bargaining. But if the prosecution then, once in court, shows only the recording of the scene in which the defendant signed the statement without showing how the plea bargaining unfolded behind closed doors, video recording of interrogations would actually work to the accused's disadvantage even more than the system currently in place.

The reason the Ministry of Justice is opposed to complete video recording of interrogations is because many prosecutors who actually conduct interrogations are of the opinion that full video recording would make it difficult to undertake interrogations of the kind possible until now and lead to an increase in crime. While I can understand how full recording of interrogations might upset prosecutors, it is a stretch of the imagination to assume any relevance in terms of its increasing, or decreasing, crime.

As the Ashikaga case also brought to light, interrogations are recorded on audio tape. If these were made public, the current situation could be expected to change, because if it became known that the prosecution had conducted coercive interrogations, presiding judges and lay judges would surely have unfavorable impressions of such prosecutors.

Statements written by prosecutors invariably begin with a remark to the effect that in advance of conducting his interrogation the prosecutor had duly informed the accused that he was not required to state anything against his own will, and that the accused had thus made the statement voluntarily.

In all my interrogations, on no occasion whatsoever was I ever given such notification. Were such notifications carried out thoroughly, prosecutors would be hard-put to draw up statements containing false content. The person being interrogated too, were he notified in advance that he had the right not to say anything he wished not to say, would not give in so easily to any statement against his will. This, if adopted in tandem with showing videos of interrogations in court, would decrease the number of convictions of innocent people markedly.

In my trial, an inordinate amount of time was spent in conjunction with the issue of the credibility and voluntariness of my statements. At the outset of the trial, Prosecutor Norio Munakata indicated that the trial would go smoothly if the defense would admit the signed statements as evidence. My attorneys, however, would not agree, claiming that the signed statements had been drawn up under threats and sugar-coated promises and therefore did not correctly reflect my thoughts or the facts. It was as a result of their refusal to admit my statements as evidence that my trial dragged on at such great length.

If future reforms to the justice system usher in full video recording of interrogations as well as complete notification to the accused of his rights, prosecutors will no longer be able to draw up statements containing false content prepared by coercive means. When that happens, statements would become credible, and trials would become substantially shorter.

The Need for Full Video Recording and Time Limits on Witness Interrogations

In connection with full video recording of interrogations, complete record-ing of how statements are prepared is needed not only for the defendant himself, but also for others who are involved in his case or who stand as witnesses in court.

In addition, in order to get court proceedings under way promptly, a limit should be placed on the time allocated to interrogating witnesses dur-ing the investigation phase.

In my interrogations in the Recruit case, there were very lengthy exchanges over the prosecution's offer to let me out on bail early if I would sign a statement, coupled with threats that I would be kept in detention for a long time if I refused. Thinking I would not be able to tolerate a lengthy detention, I ended up acquiescing to the prosecutors' demands and signed the statements they wrote whenever they instructed me to.

I was not alone. There were also officers and department heads at Recruit who underwent interrogations until late at night, day after day, until they ultimately gave in and signed statements contrary to the facts.

Naotaka Ida, my successor as Recruit president, was one. Interrogated as a witness, he underwent questioning nearly every day, from six p.m. until midnight, for close to a hundred days on end. Recruit was able to weather the crisis because, instead of a pyramid type organization, we had adopted the Peter Drucker project management system. Had Recruit been a company where all decisions were rendered by the president, it would surely have fallen into a management crisis.

Seigo Abe, who was in charge of Recruit advertising sales, was another. He was summoned on no fewer than fifty occasions, each interrogation lasting several hours. The prosecution was relentless in pressing him to make declarations in line with the claim that Ida had said he visited Fuji-nami to express gratitude for what the chief cabinet secretary had done after my visit. At the 311th session of my trial, Abe testified that although he had indeed accompanied Ida to see Fujinami that day, he had been out of earshot at the time and did not hear what Ida had said. Abe further testifiedthat he had become so exhausted from his interrogations that when the interrogating prosecutor forced him, he had put his signature to a statement written exactly as the prosecutor wanted it.

To achieve a prompt start to court proceedings, interrogations of witnesses during the investigation phase should be limited to, at most, about five hours per witness. Otherwise, not only will the people interrogated continue to become so thoroughly exhausted to the point that they will sign statements contrary to the facts, but also lay judges will not have enough time to view the videos of all the interrogations.

Witnesses should not be interrogated over long protracted periods, and their interrogations should be fully recorded on video. Doing so, I believe, will enhance the credibility of their statements and enable accurate judgments to be made.

Abolish Sentencing Demands on Indictment

In the interrogation room, time and again my prosecutors told me that if I would sign the statement placed before me, they would lighten the sentence they had asked for at the time of my indictment, adding that doing so would be sure to get me a suspended sentence. From what I was told by Kyuzaburo Hino, one of my attorneys, it is standard practice for the prosecutor in charge of an investigation to inform the prosecutor in charge of the trial what is deemed an appropriate sentence when the defendant is indicted. According to Hino, in many cases this is then used as the final sentence demanded by the prosecution.

The prosecution's offer to lighten the sentence demanded at the time of indictment if the accused signs a statement is tantamount to plea bargaining conducted in the interrogation room—plea bargaining working to the prosecution's advantage. When I was being interrogated, I often wondered what the purpose of a trial is if the prosecution's final sentencing demand is identical to what it called for at the time of indictment.

Some members of the legal profession refer to a trial as a "living organism." During a trial, there are times when, in the course of exchanges between the prosecution and the defense, the truth comes to light or new evidence or testimony enters the picture. The practice of having the prosecution call for a specific sentence at the time of indictment should be abolished.

Abolish Devious Questioning

What I refer to as "devious questioning" here is the use of the following tactic: Suppose two people, A and B, are being interrogated. First, the prosecutor tells A that B issued a statement saying such-and-such, and as a result he extracts a statement from A. The prosecutor then tells B that A issued a statement saying such-and-such and extracts a statement from B. Because of the possibility that A, when told that B made a statement to such-and-such effect, might thereby feel psychologically pressured into making a false confession, this ploy is considered unlawful.

In the Recruit affair, I was interrogated on the premise that I had approached NTT Chairman Hisashi Shinto about the transfer of Recruit

Cosmos stock; however, the person I spoke to about the stock transfer was not Shinto but his secretary, Kozo Murata. Shinto said he was told nothing at all by Murata about a stock transfer.

The prosecutor, however, raged and called me a liar. "Shinto just spilled the beans! He said he was telephoned directly by you!" With that, he made me get down on my knees and beg for forgiveness. Mentally driven into a corner, I signed a statement saying that Shinto and Murata were "connected."

Murata, even after his arrest, held to his denials or remained silent. Had that statement never been wrenched from me through the prosecutor's devious questioning, Shinto would surely have been found innocent.

A friend of mine from university days, a judge, told me that devious questioning of that sort had also occurred in the so-called Shibushi case involving alleged election fraud in Kagoshima.

In that case, supporters of Shinichi Nakayama, the winner in a local assembly election in Kagoshima Prefecture in April 2003, were charged with having held four gatherings in the town of Shibushi at which they handed out liquor and cash, to the tune of 1.91 million yen, to people in attendance. Nakayama, his wife, and the residents of Shibushi were indicted on charges of violating the Public Offices Election Law. The case generated a great deal of publicity when it was subsequently alleged that the Kagoshima Prefectural Police had conducted unlawful interrogations in which they had coerced confessions through lengthy detentions, from several months to more than a year, and forcing the accused to stomp on paper on which the names of family members were written.

Of fifteen people arrested in the case, nine denied the charges but the remaining six gave statements admitting what they were accused of, leading to the arrest of Nakayama and his wife. Mrs. Nakayama was then kept in detention for 273 days and Nakayama, for no less than 395 days.

In the end, thirteen people were indicted: Nakayama and his wife on charges of bribe passing, and eleven residents of Shibushi on charges of bribe taking. Once on trial at the Kagoshima District Court, however, the six residents who had admitted to the charges against them during their interrogations switched positions and denied the charges, contending that they had been forced to make confessions in line with the scenario that had been fabricated by the police. Ultimately the six were all found innocent. Unquestionably, many of those who were arrested in the case gave statements against their will out of fear induced by their interrogations.

Any prosecutor or police officer who conducts interrogations using unlawful and devious questioning should be punished under law to a cut in salary, official reprimand, and warning. Otherwise the use of devious questioning is bound to persist.

Abolish Preliminary "Testing" of Witnesses

Witnesses who are to appear in court are summoned to the Public Prosecutors Office in advance, where they are prepared on how to answer questions prepared by the prosecutors: in other words, they rehearse their testimony. Some witnesses are actually called to undergo such practice more than once, in some cases, two or three times.

After a witness has gone through this preliminary "testing," once in the courtroom the witness proceeds to answer the questions prepared by the prosecution. In my trial, this consisted of anywhere between twenty and thirty questions, written down on paper, at each court session.

Occasionally a witness will respond to a question differently from the testing. Without batting an eyelash the prosecutor will then say to the witness that at the Public Prosecutors Office he had stated such-and-such, and he will ask the witness which response was true, the earlier one or the one just given. Almost invariably the witness will say the response quoted by the prosecutor was the correct one.

Next, a witness will often begin to explain the background behind why he had said what he did on the earlier occasion, at which point the prosecutor will typically cut him off and say that he had not asked for any explanation, so there was no need to explain. In short, what the prosecutors do is to rehearse questions and responses with a witness in advance and then, once in the courtroom, ask only those questions that will elicit responses that will help bring a guilty verdict against the defendant.

In my trial, I suspect there were times when the preliminary testing of a witness produced responses to the disadvantage of the prosecution, and the prosecution refrained altogether from asking questions of such a witness in court. Such preliminary testing is tantamount to a second interrogation designed to extract testimony favorable to the prosecution.

Preliminary testing may also be conducted by the defense attorney, but since in court it is the prosecution that is in a position to prove a defendant's guilt, in my trial the preliminary testing by the prosecution side carried overwhelmingly more weight.

The court has no knowledge of what takes place during the preliminary testing at the Public Prosecutors Office. Moreover, since testimony unfavorable to the prosecution is not likely to emerge in the courtroom, the testing system works against an earnest quest to get at the truth.

Preliminary testing of this sort skews how a trial unfolds and is one reason why, once a person is indicted in Japan, he is convicted almost 99.8 percent of the time. Abolishing such testing should, by all means, be included in any future reforms to the justice system.

Place Defendants under Oath

A friend from university days was the presiding judge in the "Kabutoyama case" of 1974. In that case, one of the witnesses who testified under oath in court was subsequently arrested on a perjury charge.

The Kabutoyama case began when a boy and girl in residence at Kabutoyama Gakuen, a facility for mentally disabled children in Nishinomiya, Hyogo Prefecture, were found dead. A staff member, a young woman named Yamada, was arrested and indicted on a charge of having murdered one of the children, although the only evidence against her was entirely circumstantial. In connection with the case, a number of witnesses, including the head of the facility, were also arrested on perjury charges. Yamada remained in the defendant's seat for a long twenty-three years, but ultimately, in 1999, the Osaka High Court ruled that she was not guilty. The testimony she had initially given, thinking she was being helpful in doing so, in the end worked against her, forcing her to endure the unenviable position of a defendant for all too long. What happened to Yamada is extremely lamentable.

When I appeared as a witness in the court trials of others, like everyone in such circumstances prior to giving testimony I read the standard oath pledging to speak "in good faith, the whole truth and nothing but the truth," and signed my name and affixed my seal to it. To avoid committing perjury, I pounded into my memory exactly what I had testified at the other, separate trials and meticulously prepared by having my defense attorney play the role of the prosecutor. I did so because I knew too well that how one answers changes according to how the prosecutor phrases his questions. When giving actual testimony before the court, I was very nervous.

During my own trial, however, it was standard practice to make statements before the court without having taken any oath. To have a witness in a trial take an oath but not have the defendant, who inherently is in a position barring him from making false statements, do likewise runs the risk of giving the judges or lay judges the mistaken impression that the defendant is lying, because it does not matter if he lies. Not having a defendant take an oath works heavily against him and makes no sense. If anyone should be made to take an oath, it is the defendant.

Having defendants take an oath would, I believe, encourage defendants to give honest responses in court out of fear of additional charges being filed against them for perjury. If found guilty on that count, the penalty should not be light.

Abolish Lengthy Detentions

In autumn 1998, I received an invitation to dinner from an old friend, Hirotomo Takei.

Takei was the founder of the publishing firm today known as Tokuma
Shoten, after Takei sold the company to Yasuyoshi Tokuma and went into
the real estate business, establishing what became Chisan Co., Ltd. In
1992, then in his seventies, Takei was arrested on suspicion of violating the
Income Tax Act. He received a four-year prison sentence.

Over dinner, Takei told me about his experience during incarceration.
There was significant difference between life in the detention center and
that in prison—prison being considerably better. Food in prison consisted
of the likes of rice mixed with barley and daikon radish leaves cooked
in lard, but he said what was best about life in prison, as opposed to the
detention center, was the freedom to move about as one liked and be able
to look up and see sky. Every morning there was a routine of calisthenics, and once a month there was entertainment—a movie or play or something—and once a year there was a field day.

"Given my advanced age, they put me in charge of the prison library,"
he said. "But since the only time anyone came in to borrow something was
during the lunch break or in the evening, I had a lot of free time, which I
used to paint." He added that the only thing he had to be careful of was
not to get on the wrong side of the guards, whom prisoners had to call
"sir." Takei gave me a set of paintings he had created during his incarceration, and they are magnificent.

In autumn 2004, I was visited by Haruki Kadokawa, the publisher and
film director.

Kadokawa had been arrested in August 1993 on charges of smuggling
cocaine into the country. He was released on bail in December 1994. The
Lower Court handed down a four-year prison sentence which he subsequently appealed, but his appeals were rejected and he spent more than
two years in prison—from November 2001 until his release on parole in
April 2004.

When we met, Kadokawa looked hale and hearty. Like Takei, he said life
in prison had been much easier than being in detention. Shortly afterward,
Kadokawa made a complete comeback with the success of his newly pro-

duced film, *Yamato: The Last Battle*. His is a rare case of a prominent businessman who successfully staged a comeback after serving time in prison.

I cannot speak of life in prison, but from my own experience in the Tokyo Detention Center, I can say that the living environment there is truly appalling. What I found most difficult to endure was not being able to move around freely.

With the exception of morning exercises and calisthenics at three in the afternoon, I had to sit still the entire time I was in my cell. There were, among the detainees at the center, inmates serving prison time. They had to perform tasks like carrying food, dispensing meals, and cleaning the central courtyard. Watching them busily going about their jobs, I was overcome with envy at their freedom of movement.

Birds, fish, dogs—they all move about freely. All living creatures have a cerebral cortex that sustains life, with the paleocortex generating signals that control physical movements, sleep, and response to the surrounding situation. When this brain activity is suppressed, it causes dysfunction of the autonomic nervous system. In some cases, it also results in mental instability in which the sufferer cannot return to normal.

Personality changes during detention would be reduced if those who are held on a charge were allowed freedom of movement in a space at least three *tatami* mats (around 4.86 square meters) in size.

In Japan, the police and prosecutors employ what has been criticized by the nation's bar associations as "justice by hostage-taking." The accused party is taken hostage, detained until the prosecutors can obtain statements that will enable the courts to find him guilty. The distress caused by detention can be understood only by those who have actually experienced it. This is a situation I think few of my fellow countrymen are aware of.

I once saw a banner hanging on the façade of the Bar Associations Building calling for the realization of early releases on bail after indictments. It is something I personally believe in.

In my case, I was detained for 113 days, and after my release on bail I was diagnosed by a psychiatrist to be suffering from depression induced by confinement. It took nearly a year for me to feel at all normal. Within the Ministry of Justice there are medical officers, and the police authorities have teams to deal with psychological issues; so I think they are well aware that long detentions cause these serious problems. I would hope they do not take them lightly.

In relation to this, I would also like to see detainees have the option of being prescribed anti-depressants.

"Donation of Atonement"

During his trial, Hirotomo Takei made a "donation of atonement" to a correctional facility to help convicts fresh out of prison integrate back into society. Donations of atonement are monetary contributions made to groups acting in the public interest by persons who have committed offenses in which there are no victims—traffic violators whose action did not result in an accident, tax evaders, drug users, etc.—or perpetrators of crimes in which an out-of-court settlement with the victim is not possible, in order to express their remorse or atonement.

According to one of my attorneys, generally the courts make allowances when a donation of atonement is made by someone who has no financial leverage but scrapes the funds together by various means. Only rarely, however, do they extend the same mitigating courtesy in recognition of a donation made by a person who is economically privileged.

In recent years the incidence of crimes has been increasing and the recidivism rate is trending upward. Receiving any donation of atonement can make a difference for a convict returning to society. In cases where there is no victim, a donation of atonement by the perpetrator, using his own assets after meeting his tax obligations, should be recognized as reason for reducing his sentence.

Make Court Photos Public

According to media coverage, a total of 2,382 persons queued up for a chance at one of the fifty-eight seats in the visitors' gallery at the nation's first trial by lay judges, which opened on August 3, 2009.

This was extraordinary. In the past, a trial almost never attracted would-be observers in such numbers. I imagine that among those standing in line were people who wanted to use the occasion as a preview in the event they themselves were called to serve as a lay judge, as well as those who just wanted to see what a trial by lay judges was all about. One way or the other, the high level of public interest in the new justice system is not a bad thing.

Japanese people, I think, have very little knowledge about their nation's trial system. Many people might even have the impression that trials are conducted in secret, behind closed doors. One reason for this may be the fact that in Japan, photographing court proceedings is prohibited. News agencies and television stations normally take photos inside the courtroom prior to the start of proceedings, and these are shown on news programs, but photographers are required to exit the courtroom before the defendant appears. As a result, court proceedings as shown in the media are illustrated by sketches of the defendant and witnesses done by artists specializing in this area. But unlike photographs, which are objective, courtroom sketches inevitably reflect the subjective view of the artist who creates them.

Although news reporters are on hand to observe the proceedings, by profession their mission is to write articles that will pique the reader's interest. Consequently, their articles are similarly inevitably tinged by the subjective view of the writer.

In the United States, there are "court channels" on television devoted to broadcasting actual court sessions, enabling viewers to observe trials from their own living room. Today, with the growth of the Internet perhaps it is time for viewers in Japan too to be able to watch court proceedings live, in a quest toward achieving an open judicial system. It would be necessary of course to obtain the permission of those whose privacy rights are involved, but if such permission were forthcoming, I think the country would benefit from disclosure of court photos and court proceedings. People would have the opportunity to gain an understanding of how the nation's trials are conducted as well as the punishments are meted out for particular crimes. This wisdom could also serve as a deterrent to crime.

Confinement: A Lighter Sentence than Incarceration?

An acquaintance of mine used to work as a bus driver in Iwate. His younger brother caused a traffic accident and was sentenced to two years of confinement in a "traffic prison," a facility for persons who commit serious offenses as a result of a traffic violation. By the time he was released, he had undergone a complete personality change, was unable to hold a conversation, and had lost the will to work. We hired him at Appi Highland to do odd jobs. He was a very good-natured soul, but one evening he hit a pedestrian at a rural intersection where there was no traffic signal. This time he was confined to traffic prison for a year and a half. When he emerged, he was, again, a totally different person, altogether enervated and apathetic.

As human beings, we have an inborn desire to move and to exert ourselves. There is something very odd about the notion that a sentence of confinement—that confining someone to a tiny room and forbidding him to engage in any physical movement—is lighter than a prison sentence.

Consideration for Disabled Persons

Former Prime Minister Morihiro Hosokawa and his wife Kayoko were avid skiers who frequented Appi Highland, the ski resort owned by Recruit, where I got to know them. Mrs. Hosokawa served as chairperson of the Special Olympics held after the Winter Games in Nagano in 2004, and she remains involved in activities to promote self-reliance for persons with handicaps through sports. She lamented that Japan lagged behind the United States and Europe in consideration for the physically disabled.

Nobuyuki Tsujii, the first Japanese to win the Van Cliburn International Piano Competition, in 2009, happens also to be blind. In a television interview, he indicated that he had learned many a music score in Braille. If music scores exist in Braille, then why shouldn't statements and trial records be prepared in Braille? In cases when a defendant is visually impaired, a Braille specialist should be present during the interrogation to ensure communication and understanding. Similarly, when a defendant is hearing impaired, a sign-language interpreter should be present both in the interrogation room and in the courtroom.

Former Prime Minister Yukio Hatoyama espoused a political platform centered on the concept of "fraternal love." In his general policy speech after taking office, he declared his intention to review ways to support self-reliance by the disabled. Along with this political reform, under the new judicial system considerations should also be given to physically disabled individuals.

Court Interpretation

On January 27, 2000, the morning edition of the *Asahi Shimbun* reported on the trial of Govinda Prasad Mainali, a Nepalese citizen charged with the murder of a female employee of Tokyo Electric Power Company. The closing remarks by the defense, who claimed the defendant was innocent, and the voice of the interpreter filled the courtroom, in alternating succession, for nearly four hours. The verdict, the paper said, would be handed down three months later, and the writer quoted the interpreter as saying that his task would be even more demanding on that subsequent occasion because he would not have access to court documents in advance. Unquestionably, a court interpreter has to be qualified to perform duties on a level considerably higher than that of ordinary interpretation.

The *Asahi* also contained a report on court interpreters and the inability of the system to keep pace with increasing demand for them.

*With the sharp increase in cases in which a foreigner is the defen-
dant, demand for court interpreters has also increased. According to
the Supreme Court, whereas in 1989 interpretation was needed in
only one percent of all trials, today the figure has risen to over ten
percent. . . .*

*The position of interpreters is unstable. In the courthouse there
is no room or other place to which they can retire, and they are bur-
dened with the worry that if they were to register any complaint or
dissatisfaction, they might not get subsequent work.*

*In the United States, interpreter certification systems have been
introduced in some states that attract and guarantee the status of high-
quality interpreters in certain languages. The Supreme Court, however, has not shown positive support for introducing such systems,
claiming that doing so is unrealistic at the present time given the number of certified interpreters that could actually be secured nationwide.*

*Ms. (Hiromi) Nagao (Assistant Professor at Seiwa College and
president of CROSSINDEX Corp.) pleads that the matter directly
impacts the human rights of foreigners. "A system of court interpretation must be set up in order to enable foreign defendants who don't
speak Japanese to counterargue, defend themselves, and fully participate in their trial."*

Today, while more than ten percent of all trials require language interpretation, the courts are said to suffer from an insufficient number of qualified court interpreters. If the situation continues, sooner or later this can be
expected to impede trial proceedings.

In recent years, to fill the need for caregivers in Japan, the government
has begun accepting caregivers from Indonesia and the Philippines who
have undergone Japanese language education. If Japan accepts a labor
force of this nature on large scale going forward, many instances of trouble
between such caregivers and the Japanese they serve can be expected, and
serious cases could conceivably take place as well.

Globally, economies and cultures are becoming increasingly intertwined. In Tokyo and Yokohama, one in every fifty people in the workforce is a foreigner: Chinese, Korean, Indian, etc. In view of this, the number of court interpreters is far too few.

For Japan, as a major industrialized nation, it is important, given the current circumstances, to set up a system comparable to that in the United States and to boost the number of court interpreters. At the same time, because court interpretation differs from general interpretation and requires legal knowledge, there would also seem to be a need to create an institution for training court interpreters. This is no small matter, because the disposition of human life depends on whether or not accurate communication is possible during any legal procedure.

Compared to trials that involve Japanese only, in trials that require the services of a court interpreter, proceedings can be expected take at least twice as long in order to achieve accuracy in communication. The same would hold true in cases involving individuals who are blind or deaf. As such, at least six days, if not more, should be set aside for such trials, so as to afford the defendants equal treatment under the law.

Hiromasa Ezoe. Born in 1936. Graduated in educational psychology from the University of Tokyo. Established Daigaku Kokoku Co. Ltd., the predecessor of today's Recruit Co., Ltd., 1960. Launched the Ezoe Scholarship Society Foundation, 1971. Resigned as chairman of Recruit, 1988.

Has served as chairman of the Ezoe Scholarship Society Foundation and director for La Voce Incorporated, which promotes opera and classical music performances. Published Where Is the Justice?: Media Attacks, Prosecutorial Abuse, and My 13 Years in Japanese Court *in English from Kodansha International, 2010.*

IV

THE LIGHT AND DARK SIDES OF JAPAN'S NEW LAY JUDGE SYSTEM

Shozaburo Ishida, Attorney at Law

Japan's new judicial system calling for the participation of lay judges in criminal trials went into effect on May 21, 2009, still fraught with a multitude of problems. It continues to be used in real court trials.

Launched on the pretext of having ordinary citizens participate in the administration of justice, the system is destined to drag the country's already hopeless criminal trial process into an even deeper abyss.

The State of Affairs

The lay judge system was created to get ordinary Japanese citizens involved in specific phases of the criminal justice process: namely, the trial proceedings, deliberations, and delivery of a verdict.

In the latter two phases, judgments are rendered in two broad areas: determination of the facts in the case and deciding on the appropriate sentence.

Finding the facts of a case translates to judging whether the accused is innocent or guilty. Strictly speaking, it is judging whether or not the contentions made by the prosecution—the charges recorded in the indictments—have been demonstrated with absolute certainty, that is, whether or not the prosecution has succeeded in establishing the accused's guilt beyond a reasonable doubt.

After World War II, Japan adopted a new system for prosecuting criminal cases. Since that time, the trial of a defendant has been conducted first in a district court in the presence of one judge or a trio of judges working as a team.

All of the nation's judges are qualified legal professionals attached to a national institution. Although Japan embraces the principle of the separation of powers, until now trials have been conducted only by judges affiliated with a national institution.

Under the new lay judge system, the facts of a case are determined and the appropriate punishment weighed by, in principle, nine individuals: three judges by profession and six ordinary citizens serving as lay judges. Although the inclusion of ordinary citizens in the judicial process is departure from the way things were done, in fact this is not the first time that Japanese citizens have taken part in the nation's criminal trials. It is not widely known that, during the short span of fifteen years—from 1928, when the Jury Act enacted in 1923 went into effect, until 1943, when legislation terminated the Act's implementation—Japan conducted trials by a jury made up of twelve members. The legislation of 1923 stipulated that when the war was over the jury system was to be reinstated, but this never happened. It took more than six decades before trials by jury reappeared, this time in the form of the lay judge system.

Trials applicable to the lay judge system are those in which the accused, if found guilty, would be sentenced either to death or life imprisonment, or those in which the sentence would be short—one year or longer—although the accused had brought about the victim's death by willful act. Applicable cases include murder, robbery resulting in death or injury, arson of an inhabited structure, kidnapping for ransom, dangerous negligence resulting in death, and bodily injury resulting in death. To begin, the accused is found guilty or not guilty by a majority among the nine judges. In the case of a guilty verdict, the proper punishment is weighed and determined, again, by a majority vote. To pass a ruling disadvantageous to the accused, at least one of the three court judges must be included in the majority.

Introduction of a lay judge system of this kind was first suggested in June 2001 in "For a Justice System to Support Japan in the 21st Century," a set of recommendations prepared by the Justice System Reform Council under the leadership of the Jun'ichiro Koizumi Cabinet. The following is a translation from the Supreme Court website on the reasons for the system's introduction:

> Until now, in conducting criminal trials, because of the court's excessive importance attached to specialized accuracy, deliberations and verdicts have often been difficult for the average citizen to understand; also, in some cases, deliberations dragged on over long durations, and for these reasons the impression may have been given that criminal trials are not easily approached. Also, in many nations today systems have been created to involve citizens directly in the criminal trial process, and doing so is playing a significant role in deepening citizens' understanding of how justice is administered. In this light, among the latest reforms to the justice system, introducing a system whereby the nation's citizens would participate in the judicial process was taken under consideration, and a system of lay judges was proposed under which judges and lay judges selected from the general populace would pool their respective knowledge and experience to render judgments, in the belief that through this collaboration a trial system could be achieved that will be more readily understandable by the nation's citizens.

Until now, for many people criminal trials have been events to be read about in the newspaper or watched on television, that is, they have been affairs that did not involve them personally. But with the introduction of the lay judge system, in a sense criminal trials may indeed become affairs close to home.

A variety of measures have also been devised to achieve trials that are faster and easy to understand. But can it be said that the lay judge system will bring suitable benefit to those who serve as lay judges or to the accused party on trial—and by extension to society as a whole? Are we truly doing the right thing in promoting the advancement of this system?

Realizing trials more readily understandable to the nation's citizens through their participation in the administration of justice is the "light" side of the system. But while this itself may be a noble cause, I cannot help thinking this light aspect is enfolded by a great "dark" side that is less evident.

Criminal Trial Formats and the Lay Judge System

Formats of Criminal Trials

With the introduction of the lay judge system, the misconception has formed that Japan has now joined the ranks of nations that adopt a system of trials by jury.

To assume that introducing the lay judge system will lead to stories with dramatic endings in which common citizens do battle against authority in the deliberation process—stories of the kind portrayed in films like *12 Angry Men* (1957) and *The Verdict* (1982)—is a grave mistake.

The lay judge system is a system that has similarities to but is ultimately quite different from trials by jury or trials by judge and jury as seen elsewhere.

Participation by citizens in criminal trials in countries around the world broadly divides into two formats: trial by jury and trial by judge and jury. The general differences between the two are shown in Table 1. As indicated, there are four major differences:

— How citizens are selected for participation in deliberations;
— Whether or not the defendant has the right to choose under which system he will be tried;
— Whether or not professional judges participate in discussions concerning the verdict; and
— Whether or not a verdict must be unanimous.

Normally, in the system of trials by jury, only jury members engage in determination of the facts and judges weigh the punishment.

In a trial by judge and jury, jury members and judges form a joint panel

TABLE 1 Criminal Trial Systems

	Term of duty for Judge-Jury	Selectable by defendant	Fact-finding	Sentencing	Participation of judge(s)	Deliberations
Jury (1:12)*	1 case only	Yes	Yes	No (in some states, Yes)	No	Unanimous decision required (in some states, 10 out of 12 votes will suffice) (in case of hung jury, retrial required)
Judge-Jury (1:2 or 3:2)	Specified no. of days	No	Yes	Yes	Yes	2/3 majority
Lay judge (3:6)	1 case only	No	Yes	Yes	Yes	Majority

* Ratio of court judges to jury members/judge-jury members/lay judges

Countries adopting jury system: Austria, Belgium, Brazil, Denmark, El Salvador, Ireland, Mexico, Nicaragua, Panama, Spain, United Kingdom, United States, etc. (Data shown refers to serious crimes in principal U.S. states.)

Countries adopting judge-jury system: Australia, France, Germany, Greece, Italy, Portugal, Sweden, Venezuela, etc. (Data shown refers to Germany.)

that collectively finds the facts of the case and weighs the punishment. This system is quite similar to the system of lay judges newly adopted in Japan, with the exception of a significant difference in the methods by which citizens are appointed to serve. In Germany, for example, citizens are recommended by various groups and appointed to serve for a specified period of time. This resembles the method used in Japan for selecting mediation committee members, members of labor relations commissions, etc. But in contrast, jury members and lay judges in Japan are selected at random for each case.

In the lay judge system, at each district court, candidates for lay judges are first determined by lottery of citizens on voter registration lists. Around November each year, the citizens appearing on these lists are sent notifications of their listing along with questionnaires to ascertain whether or not they are professionally barred from serving as a lay judge or have an objectively acceptable reason to decline.

Next, when an indictment is issued in a case that calls for a trial by lay judges, the court chooses, again by lottery, between fifty and one hundred citizens from its list of candidates and sends candidates a letter informing them that they have become candidates to serve as a lay judge in a specified case, and requesting that they appear at the courthouse on the trial date.

On the day of the trial, the presiding judge asks each candidate whether he or she has any doubts concerning their ability to contribute to a fair trial and whether they wish to decline, and if so, their reasons for doing so. Finally, six lay judges are chosen for the case.

The differences between the civil judge system and the jury system are important characteristics impacting how criminal trials are carried out. To overlook this point and stress only that citizens participate in the judicial process is to argue without paying heed to the essence of the system. Doing so can bring tragic results for both the citizens who participate and for the defendant who must undergo such a trial.

Problems for Lay Judges
Obligation to serve as a lay judge

Article 18 of the Constitution of Japan states that "involuntary servitude . . . is prohibited." Article 19 stipulates: "Freedom of thought and conscience shall not be violated."

In this context, the first problem for citizens is that, unless they have a specific reason to decline, they are compelled, as a legal obligation, to appear in court as a candidate for, and to serve as, a lay judge.

Candidates for service as lay judges receive notification and a questionnaire by mail. However, from the point when candidates receive a summons to appear at the courthouse on a specified date, they become subject to criminal penalties should certain obligations not be met. For example, if the candidate is found to have returned the questionnaire with any false information, a fine is imposed in an amount up to 500,000 yen. The same applies if, on the date the candidate is to appear at the courthouse, false statements are made to the judge. If a candidate refuses to answer questioning without justifiable cause, he may be subject to receiving a non-penal fine.

If a candidate fails to appear at the courthouse on the appointed date without justifiable cause, a non-penal fine is imposed. Acceptable reasons for declining include protracted overseas business trips, a busy time of year for farmers, caregiving, pregnancy, etc.; however, it is up to the court to judge whether or not these reasons are justifiable in the instance at hand. Not wanting to stand in judgment of others, not wishing to be involved in a trial that might eventuate in a death sentence, or simply being too busy is not an acceptable reason for declining to serve.

Does this not violate the stipulation of freedom of conscience guaranteed in the Constitution?

Confidentiality

Another weighty obligation is imposed on those who become lay judges and become involved in a court trial: the obligation to maintain confidentiality. This is an obligation one must shoulder one's entire life, and any violation results in the imposition of a very heavy penalty.

The items concerning which absolute secrecy must be maintained are the following:

— The content of the behind-the-scenes deliberations by the judges and lay judges leading to their verdict;
— Opinions expressed by judges and lay judges, and the number of opinions constituting, respectively, the majority and minority;
— Secrets learned in the course of their duties;
— The facts thought to warrant determination, and the penalty thought to merit determination, in the case at hand; and
— The appropriateness, or otherwise, of the determination of facts indicated, and of the penalty determined, in the verdict at hand.

Those who become lay judges and become involved in a trial undergo an extremely unusual experience. It would seem only natural that they would be driven by an urge to tell others—family, friends, etc.—about it. And it is also conceivable they would not be able to ignore the media's relentless onslaught to interview them. Moreover, in the event that the opinions expressed by lay judges during the deliberations of the case were ignored and the court reached a conclusion by coercion, it would be in the public interest that this be made known.

The rules governing such matters, however, stipulate that a lay judge can be penalized for saying to others such things as:

"I felt sorry for the defendant."

"Other lay judges shared my view."

"I thought the defendant was innocent."

"I felt a suspended sentence was appropriate, but an unsuspended sentence was decided by a close vote of five to four."

"The young judge was of the same opinion as me."

"The judge used coercive means to bring about a guilty verdict."

In the United States, basically once one's jury duty is over, the content of what the jury deliberated can be made public. In the famous trial of O.J. Simpson in the United States, for example, after the trial the members of the jury were interviewed by the press and each gave detailed accounts of the course of their deliberations.

It might be mentioned here that in Japan judges too are, under Article 75 of the Court Act, obligated to maintain secrecy concerning deliberations, but no penalties are stipulated. Once a judge retires from his office, he is no longer under such obligation.

The reason such an obligation was imposed on lay judges was undoubtedly the fear that the public would learn what the judges said and did during deliberations.

There is absolutely no need to impose such a harsh obligation on lay judges.

Execution of punitive powers and citizen participation

The next problem is that the lay judge system is a system that seeks to get citizens involved in a state institution that wields authoritative powers.

Clearly, criminal trials ultimately lead to the execution of punitive powers by the state. In other words, it is a typical way for the state to exercise its authority against the nation's citizens. The lay judge system is a move to have citizens shoulder part of that burden.

Until now, whenever a verdict was handed down that raised eyebrows, criticism took the form of censure of the court, a state institution. Now, with verdicts reached with the participation of lay judges, responsibility for any odd or questionable verdicts will be shifted to citizens, marked by a sense that since citizens were included any questionable verdicts should simply be accepted with resignation. In short, citizens have been relegated to carrying the burden of being an alibi for the judges.

Will the Defendant's Human Rights Be Protected?

Requirement to Undergo Trial by Lay Judges

Article 37 of the Constitution of Japan states that "in all criminal cases the accused shall enjoy the right to a speedy and public trial by an impartial tribunal."

The problem is that all defendants who have been indicted for specific crimes are required to undergo a trial by lay judges. Defendants cannot choose to be tried by a court of judges alone.

In the United States, according to its Constitution, undergoing a trial by jury is a right, not an obligation. Amendment 6 stipulates: "In all criminal prosecutions, the accused shall enjoy the right to a speedy and public trial, by an impartial jury." The accused has the right to renounce that right, and a trial is opened only after the accused has declared his innocence. About half of those who go on trial opt to be tried by a jury. According to statistics for the federal district courts, in the year 2007, of 7,849 trials conducted that year, 3,213, or roughly forty percent, were trials by jury.

In Japan, however, under the new lay judge system a defendant must undergo a trial by lay judges whether he wants to or not. For this reason, a number of arguments concerning the system are being debated: for example, the fact that the Japanese Constitution makes no stipulations in anticipation of trials by judge-and-jury, or whether trials involving lay judges can be said to be fair, or whether the system violates judges' independence.

Debates like these aside, anyone indicted on charges of certain designated crimes are now required to undergo a trial by lay judges. There is no choice in the matter. Why such individuals must undergo a trial by lay judges without any other options open to them is a question that leaves grave doubts.

Restrictions on the Accused's Right of Defense

The most serious problem is that in order to implement the lay judge system an array of measures were taken to restrict the defendant's right of defense.

In a nutshell, the possibility exists that in a rush to complete a trial, a mistaken verdict might be handed down. The issues are these:

- Pre-trial procedures place limitations on the claims that can be made and on the evidence that can be submitted.
- The lay judge selection process is completed in half a day. Is it possible to select impartial lay judges within such a short time frame?
- Trials are to be completed within three days normally, and within seven days at the most. Rather than "speedy," is this not "hasty"?
- Can fairness be maintained with judges taking part in deliberations?
- Could a verdict based on a majority vote be an infringement of the principles of criminal trials?
- Will appellate trials become mere formalities?
- Is it appropriate to entrust lay judges with the judgment of weighing punishments?

Pre-trial Procedures

The first three items listed above are said to be measures implemented to keep the burden off the lay judges.

In particular, pre-trial procedures are a system newly added to the Code of Criminal Procedure with the lay judge system in mind. Stated concisely, the system makes advance preparations for a trial by requiring the defendant's claims and evidence to be pared down before the start of the trial.

The contentions of the prosecution are clarified, and the counter arguments are also clarified in advance. The prosecution discloses necessary evidence to the defense, time is provided to mull over the evidence, and necessary witnesses and/or evidence are gathered.

On the surface this system looks favorable, but speaking from my long years of experience as a defense attorney, the system is an outrage.

Criminal cases are not cut and dry. There are times when, depending on the statements made by a witness or the evidence found during the course of the trial, a trial can move in a totally different direction.

Under the lay judge system, however, because a verdict must be handed down within three to five days, the possibility exists that, barring extenuating circumstances, it may become impossible to submit any evidence other than that which was decided upon during the pre-trial procedures.

In one case I was involved in, a case ultimately found to have involved false charges, nine people were accused of having committed a series of three crimes: two attacks by explosion attempted (one successfully) in October and November 1969, the Nippon Oil Building post office explosion of October 1971 that I described in chapter 2, and a similar explosion at the house of an officer of the National Health Insurance program in December 1971. It took nine years to prove the defendants were innocent.

In the aforementioned O.J. Simpson case in the United States, which began in June 1994, jury selection took nearly four months, the trial began in January 1995 and continued over a span of 265 days, until a ruling was handed down on October 3, and more than 120 witnesses were interrogated. During the trial, 24 jury members and alternates were apparently sequestered in a hotel. In the United States, getting at the truth doesn't seem to allow for the convenience of the jury members.

One must conclude that under a system like the lay judge system, viewed from the perspective of the defendant, undergoing a hasty trial in order to accelerate procedures puts them at an extreme disadvantage.

Decisions by Majority Vote

Another question is the appropriateness for a verdict to be decided by a majority vote.

In dubio pro reo, the legal term that loosely translates as "when there is an element of doubt, decide in favor of the accused," often comes up in reference to criminal trials. It concisely expresses the principle that only when the prosecution's contentions are proven to be absolutely correct can the defendant be found guilty and a verdict be handed down against him.

Individuals who are chosen to be lay judges are given the following instructions from the court: "Although it is impossible to confirm directly whether facts took place in the past, there are instances when, in the course of everyday life even, judgments are made as to whether or not something actually took place, based on what people involved say and so on. In a court trial, however, a person cannot be penalized for something that is uncertain, and a defendant is found guilty only when, after examining the evidence, it is thought, based on common sense, that the defendant unquestionably committed the crime of which he is accused in the indictment. On the other hand, if, based on common sense, there is doubt concerning his guilt, he must be found innocent."

What these instructions say is that unless the prosecution proves the defendant's guilt *beyond a reasonable doubt*, the accused cannot be found guilty. In other words, so long as reasonable doubt exists, a verdict of innocence must be handed down.

"I don't think the prosecution's claims make sense."

"I don't think one could call the evidence 'conclusive.'"

"There's definitely something suspicious about the defendant, but the possibility could exist that he isn't the culprit."

Only when doubts of these kinds have all been erased can a judgment of guilt be passed against a defendant.

If this way of thinking is not adhered to at all times, the possibility exists of a wrongful conviction: finding an innocent person guilty of a crime he did not commit.

Use of the article "a" in "beyond a reasonable doubt" merits special notice. It signifies that even if *a single doubt* remains, a defendant cannot be found guilty.

In the American trial by jury system, with the exception of a few states, a verdict in a criminal trial cannot be reached unless all twelve jury members are in complete agreement. If even one jury member opposes the conclusion reached by the other eleven, a "hung jury" results and a retrial is ruled. In other words, if even one jury member thinks there is something dubious, it is taken to mean that the prosecution has failed to prove the defendant's guilt *beyond a reasonable doubt.*

In Japan, however, the lay judge system has been devised in such a way that a verdict can be handed down on the basis of a simple majority.

What this means is that, in an extreme case, even if four of the six lay judges harbor doubts, it is still possible for a defendant to be found guilty if the three judges vote the other way, resulting in a five-against-four tally. It is highly dubious whether a system such as this can be said to be in line with the principles of criminal trial law.

Sentencing

Sentencing is the process by which a decision is reached on the appropriate degree of punishment to be meted out to a defendant who has been found guilty. It is the final phase of the nation's exercise of its right to impose criminal punishment.

Because a sentence has a life-changing impact on a defendant, weighing a fit sentence is a heavy responsibility that requires a high level of legal knowledge and experience. Under the lay judge system, however, lay judges—common citizens—are made to participate in the decision weighing an appropriate sentence.

Under Japanese criminal law, the rules on sentencing are extremely broad. As an example, Article 199 of the Criminal Code of Japan, which applies to crimes of homicide, states: "A person who kills another shall be punished by the death penalty or imprisonment with work for life or for a definite term of not less than five years." Thus, the minimum legal punishment for homicide is a prison term of five years. However, if the defendant is found to have extenuating circumstances, the court has authority to reduce his sentence. There are also cases where, depending on the circumstances involved, a sentence can be suspended for a set amount of time. When extenuating circumstances apply, the sentence can be reduced by up to one-half, yielding a sentence of two years and six months. In such cases, because the sentence is less than three years, it can, depending on the circumstances, be suspended.

Accordingly, in cases when a defendant is found guilty of homicide, the punishment can span an extremely wide range—from the death penalty all the way to a two-and-a-half-year suspended sentence. From this broad range, a choice must be made as to what is deemed the most appropriate punishment to fit the crime, taking various circumstances into consideration. This is not a judgment that can be easily reached—especially since it is a matter affecting a human being's entire life. Is it right to delegate this task, the determination of fit punishment, to common citizens who have no experience in such matters whatsoever?

To begin with, ample thought must be given to various matters when meting out punishment. What meaning is there in the state's imposing punishment on a person convicted of a crime? How should the state go about exercising its right to punish? Specifically, is punishment meted out to serve as revenge on behalf of the victim, or for the purpose of educating the person who committed the crime and getting him to reform his ways?

To leave the decision on sentencing to everyday citizens, whose awareness of such basic issues is hazy at best, is extremely problematical not just for the defendant as one might expect, but also for the lay judges as well. In particular, to make citizens rule on matters of life and death—whether or not a defendant should be sentenced to death—is to place an extremely heavy burden upon the shoulders of lay judges.

Personally, I oppose capital punishment. If I were in charge of the defense in a trial of this nature in the near future, in my closing argument I would look deep into the eyes of each lay judge in turn and say this:

"As lay judges, you have blamed the defendant of having killed someone. I too believe that as a human being the greatest act of evil is to kill someone, no matter what the reasons might be. Just now the prosecution has asked for the death penalty. They are asking you to take the life of the defendant. This is tantamount to telling you to kill someone while simultaneously declaring that murder is an act of evil. No matter how legal it might be, capital punishment is no different from homicide. If, in rendering your verdict, you vote to impose the death penalty, you will be abetting the taking of a human life—the most unacceptable act that can be performed as a human being. Do you still want to vote for the death penalty? I ask you, please, to think the matter over thoroughly one more time."

Momentous issues are thus thrust upon the lay judges.

Criminal Trials in Crisis

All systems have their light and dark sides. The fact of the matter is that, so long as they are the workings of human beings, no system can be one-hundred-percent ideal. However, in instances when it is clear that the source of a malady from which recovery is difficult exists in the dark area covering the light, history teaches us that unless that source is excised quickly, the disease will inevitably spread and slowly come to affect the light area as well. Here, the malady is the lay judge system.

I believe that until this point almost no one has taken great interest in the nation's judicial system, especially criminal trials, thinking it was something that did not affect them. In that respect, it can be said that the issues surrounding the lay judge system present a perfect opportunity for each Japanese citizen to think about how criminal trials are undertaken.

How should criminal trials be carried out? What are the problems with the current lay judge system? And what can be done to resolve those problems?

To keep the lay judge system as it now exists will lead to a crisis in the Japanese criminal trial system from which it will be difficult for the nation to recover.

V

IMPACT OF THE LAY JUDGE SYSTEM ON CRIMINAL TRIALS

Masanori Ono, Attorney at Law

The Lay Judge Trial System

The lay judge system launched on May 21, 2009, is a mechanism whereby, in specified cases, court cases are now to be decided by a total of nine individuals: three professional judges and six lay judges selected from the general population. Going forward, fact-finding and sentencing in the district courts, formerly conducted by a panel of three professional judges, will be performed jointly by nine persons.

Trial proceedings consist of listening to the contentions of two sides—the prosecution and the defense—and then deciding which side's claims are correct. Although rendering such a judgment may appear difficult, what a trial actually involves is not judging which side is correct but rather judging whether or not to admit the contention of the prosecution that the defendant committed such-and-such offense.

An array of evidence is presented in court—some that support the contentions of the prosecution and some that contradict them. The issue is to examine all the evidence presented and thereupon decide whether or not what the prosecution contends is logical against the yardstick of common sense and thus correct.

If the contentions of the prosecution are admitted, the defendant is found guilty; but if there remains any doubt concerning those contentions or the prosecution's contentions have not been sufficiently proven, a guilty verdict cannot be handed down, that is, the defendant is found innocent. It is up to

the prosecution to demonstrate spot-on proof that a criminal act was committed, and if such demonstration is not fully convincing, then as a rule the defendant must be acquitted. What the court must decide is not whether or not
the contentions made by the defendant and his defense team are correct, but
rather whether the claims made by the prosecution can be said to be proven
by the evidence at hand. If, based on this principle, the nine individuals—
judges and lay judges—determine that the defendant is guilty, they then weigh
his sentencing. This is fundamentally how the lay judge trial system works.

Cases subject to trial by lay judges are stipulated under law (the Act on
Criminal Trials Examined under Lay Judge System, commonly referred to
as the "Lay Judge Act"). The target cases are those meriting, in the event
of a guilty verdict, either the death penalty or life imprisonment. Also
included are cases deserving either the death penalty, life imprisonment, or
more than one year of incarceration when the crime is premeditated and
results in the death of its victim. A description of the specific case types
these parameters apply to can be seen in Table 1.

Overall, the number of cases subject to the lay judge system has been
declining, falling from 3,800 per year in 2004 to near 2,300 in 2008.
Among such cases, robberies resulting in injury are the most numerous.
Cases of this kind refer to thefts in which a victim is physically attacked
and injured. The next most numerous are homicides. Although the number
of murders has changed little over the course of many decades, recently
they appear to be tapering off slightly.

The list, arranged by number of cases reported in 2008, continues with
arson of an inhabited building, rape resulting in death or injury, bodily
injury resulting in death, etc. All cases listed qualify as serious crimes, and
in each instance judgments are now to be rendered through trials in which
the nation's citizens participate.

Trials by lay judges are being held at district courts across the country.
Fundamentally there is one such court in each of the forty-seven prefectures, the sole exception being Hokkaido, which has four. Some prefectures
also undertake trials at court branches: for example, in Tokyo at the Tachi-
kawa Branch and in Kanagawa at the Odawara Branch.

TABLE 1 Number of cases (2004–2008) to which lay judge trial system would now be applied

Crime	Year				
	2004	2005	2006	2007	2008
Total	3,800	3,633	3,111	2,645	2,324
Robbery resulting in injury	1,146	1,111	939	695	590
Homicide	761	690	642	557	543
Arson of inhabited building, etc.	357	322	331	287	234
Rape resulting in death/injury	316	274	240	218	189
Bodily injury resulting in death	229	205	181	171	173
Indecent assault resulting in death/injury	167	132	161	168	136
Robbery-rape	197	165	153	129	125
Violation of Stimulation Drug Control Act	145	118	125	94	106
Robbery resulting in death (robbery-homicide)	136	123	72	66	86
Passage of counterfeit currency	151	244	40	62	36
Currency counterfeiting	53	76	30	17	23
Gang rape resulting in death/injury	—	14	16	23	18
Reckless driving resulting in death	38	43	56	51	17
Violation of Narcotics and Psychotropic Control Act	20	19	14	13	10
Abandonment by a person responsible for protection, resulting in death	8	8	14	10	8
Violation of Criminal Regulations to Control Explosives	6	3	1	4	8
Violation of Act for Controlling the Possession of Firearms or Swords and Other Such Weapons	23	37	40	29	6
Others	47	49	56	51	16

Note 1: Number of cases shown (crimes other than those subject to the Penal Code) refers only to cases applicable to lay judge trial system.

Note 2: Quantities are approximate numbers of cases received at district courts, subject to later changes. For defendants charged with multiple crimes, each indictment is counted as 1 case.

Table 2 shows the number of cases subject to the lay judge system listed by district court. In both 2007 and 2008, the number of such cases was highest in Osaka Prefecture, whereas in 2006 the highest number had been recorded in Tokyo. As percentages of the population, the larger numbers registered in Tokyo and Osaka are, in a sense, not surprising.

The number of cases is also significant in Chiba Prefecture, which abuts Tokyo to the east; in 2007 Chiba recorded nearly the same number of cases as Tokyo. Although the prefecture is not as populous as Tokyo, the large number of cases may in part owe to Chiba's being home to Narita International Airport. At the other end of the scale, the number of cases is modest in prefectures such as Yamagata, Toyama, Akita, Fukui, Shimane, and Ishikawa.

In the case of Tokyo, in 2008 there were 213 applicable cases. If these trials were carried out year-long, given that each case requires several days, this calculates to a trial by lay judges being convened virtually every day in one of Tokyo's district courts.

Actual figures for 2009 show that between May 21 and October 31, the number of newly indicted cases subject to trial by lay judges totaled 834 nationwide. Homicide cases topped the list at 203, followed by robberies causing injury at 179. By location, cases were most numerous in Osaka, with 91, followed by Chiba with 85 and Tokyo with 69.

Table 3 shows the number of "conventional" criminal cases (excluding traffic violations) handled by the nation's district courts in 2008: approximately 93,600. Of that total, only an extremely small number, roughly 2,300, or less than 2.5 percent, were cases that would now be subject to trial by lay judges.

A look at the figures for 2004 through 2007 reveals that in each year the number of cases that would qualify today for a trial by lay judges was near three percent of the total number of cases tried in the nation's district courts. What this means is that only a small percentages of the cases handled by local courts would actually entail a trial by lay judges.

Among all criminal cases, traffic-related cases are most numerous, but among "normal" criminal offenses (violations of the Road Traffic Law are categorized as "special law offenses") thefts account for a considerable percentage. The number of cases involving possession or use of stimulants is also fairly large.

Opposition has been voiced to the application of the lay judge trial system to cases of serious crime. Launching the system for major cases is unreasonable, opponents argue, and they suggest starting with simpler cases. Personally, however, I do not see very much meaning in applying the system to simple cases. With theft, possession of stimulants, and the like, although the facts are simple and there is a definite trend in terms of sentencing, the burden on lay judges would be weighty compared to the seriousness of those crimes.

Instead of simple crimes of that nature, the new system deals with cases that have a significant impact on society and are of great interest to people: serious cases for which it is thought to be beneficial for the opinions of the nation's citizens to be involved in the judgment process.

The lay judge trial system is, however, applied to cases involving stimulant drugs where such drugs have been imported, exported, or produced for economic gain.

Finally, Table 4 includes a figure indicating, in broad parameters, the number of days in court required for applicable cases to date.

It may seem surprising, but relatively few of the "serious" cases tried have involved lengthy battles in the courtroom. Although arguments have been waged over specific circumstances or reasons behind a crime, or over the question of whether the defendant was criminally responsible for his actions, in nearly all cases the defendant has admitted to his crime by way of confession. As such, the trials themselves have not taken an inordinate amount of time to be brought to a close. Trials that drag out tend to involve accusations of breach of trust, corporate embezzlement, fraud, bribery, etc. In the Recruit bribery case, the trial at the district court level alone took over thirteen years. Cases of these kinds are not subject to trials by lay judges, however.

Granted, among cases of serious crime that grab the public's attention there are some whose trials go on at great length. In cases that are highly

TABLE 2

Number of cases (2004–2008) to which lay judge trial system would now be applied, by district court

Court	2004	2005	2006	2007	2008
Total	3,800	3,633	3,111	2,645	2,324
Sapporo	87	75	79	70	42
Hakodate	13	9	9	23	14
Asahikawa	16	12	15	17	15
Kushiro	17	13	13	12	10
Aomori	17	27	25	17	21
Akita	15	15	15	10	9
Morioka	16	21	20	21	11
Sendai	47	63	54	61	39
Yamagata	23	21	21	17	7
Fukushima HQ	17	16	9	3	10
Koriyama Branch	21	34	33	33	33
Mito	122	99	74	42	60
Utsunomiya	64	58	52	62	50
Maebashi	91	69	60	62	27
Saitama	235	184	121	106	110
Chiba	297	276	238	214	172
Tokyo HQ	338	413	324	215	213
Tachikawa Branch	62	74	64	40	46
Yokohama HQ	228	226	161	153	99
Odawara Branch	27	28	26	18	21
Niigata	43	27	39	29	20
Toyama	34	31	17	11	7
Kanazawa	10	27	8	18	8
Fukui	9	10	13	7	9
Kofu	17	29	12	15	26
Nagano HQ	20	31	15	34	10
Matsumoto Branch	16	16	21	23	10
Gifu	45	37	46	36	40
Shizuoka HQ	25	17	23	19	12
Numazu Branch	33	59	38	25	11
Hamamatsu Branch	22	19	19	14	28

Court	Year				
	2004	2005	2006	2007	2008
Nagoya HQ	210	207	170	114	127
Okazaki Branch	65	82	46	21	29
Tsu	53	75	60	39	32
Otsu	31	40	34	13	18
Kyoto	46	72	47	70	51
Osaka HQ	351	279	298	254	218
Sakai Branch	76	48	47	52	32
Kobe HQ	112	80	100	87	73
Himeji Branch	55	36	33	21	13
Nara	35	37	27	39	28
Wakayama	35	25	19	16	20
Matsue	17	12	9	14	8
Tottori	12	11	10	11	11
Okayama	36	41	39	37	36
Hiroshima	71	52	51	37	29
Yamaguchi	25	29	33	27	14
Tokushima	21	22	18	16	14
Takamatsu	32	44	32	27	21
Matsuyama	45	32	29	16	31
Kochi	29	34	24	19	26
Fukuoka HQ	157	102	94	94	121
Kokura Branch	48	36	51	32	35
Saga	12	13	18	9	20
Nagasaki	34	31	24	22	22
Kumamoto	35	36	47	40	32
Oita	40	27	14	17	22
Miyazaki	18	32	20	18	22
Kagoshima	33	28	29	29	16
Naha	39	34	24	27	13

Note: Quantities are approximate numbers of cases received at each district court, subject to later changes. For defendants charged with multiple crimes, each indictment is counted as 1 case.

TABLE **3** Number of cases (2004–2008) to which lay judge trial system would now be applied

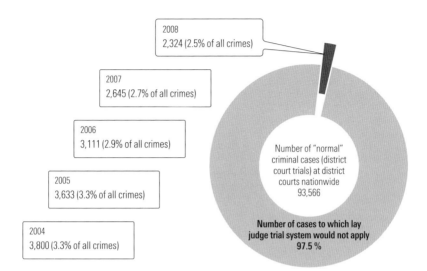

Note: Yearly totals are approximate numbers of cases received at district courts nationwide, subject to later changes. For defendants charged with multiple crimes, each indictment is counted as 1 case.

complex or in which there are many points of dispute, quite some time is necessary before a ruling is handed down. Such cases are the exception, though.

In real terms, conventional "simple" criminal trials take only one hour, from ten a.m. to eleven a.m. In nearly all instances, a verdict is passed down the same day, but the majority of cases come to a close after, at most, just several court sessions. Even with trials involving serious crimes applicable to a trial by lay judges, a considerable number end after two or three sessions; moreover, court proceedings do not continue all day but in many instances involve only a morning or afternoon session. The reason, as I will touch upon below, is because in almost all trials documents are submitted as evidence and in the courtroom their content is stated quite concisely and the proceedings close; the time spent in court is very short because the judges take the documents back to their chambers to read.

TABLE 4 Number of defendants in cases (2008) to which lay judge trial system would now be applied, current average length of court proceedings, and average number of court sessions

	Case type					
	Lay judge trial cases			Lay judge trial cases with pre-trial procedures completed		
Confessions/ denials	Number of defendants receiving final judgment	Average length of court proceedings (months)	Average number of court sessions	Number of defendants receiving final judgment	Average length of court proceedings (months)	Average number of court sessions
Total number of defendants receiving final judgment	2,208	7,7	4,3	1,788	7,1	3,5
Confessions	1,265	5,9	3,0	1,026	5,6	2,6
Denials	904	10,5	6,1	755	9,1	4,7

The reason the total number of defendants receiving final judgment does not correspond to the total of confessions and denials is because of the existence of defendants in public prosecution cases who were transferred, etc. prior to the start of presentation of statements. The figures shown refer to the actual numbers of defendants in cases where a verdict, etc. was handed down. In cases when a defendant has been given multiple indictments, this is counted as 1 actual defendant so long as the defense argument encompassed the multiple charges. The information provided here is based on data prior to the start of the lay judge trial system. In order to realize trials in which citizens can more easily participate, court proceedings are to be carried out with greater alacrity after the system begins. As a result of the launch of pre-trial procedures on November 1, 2005, the average length of court proceedings in cases applicable to the lay judge trial system, from acceptance of a case through to a final ruling, has been shortened, most remarkably in cases involving denial by the defendant. All numbers shown in the table are approximations.

Number of court sessions in cases to which the lay judge trial system would now be applied (2008, cases with pre-trial procedures)

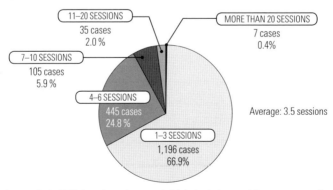

Data is based on results for 2008, i.e. prior to the start of trials by lay judges, and does not necessarily reflect how court sessions will be counted after the start of lay judge trials. In order to realize trials in which citizens can more easily participate, court proceedings are to be carried out with greater alacrity after the system begins.

On this latter point, with trials by lay judges the situation has changed. Lay judges do not take documents back to their "rooms" in the courthouse to read; instead they render their judgments based on the evidence investigated in the courtroom. Even so, in cases involving no particular points in dispute, trials will generally close after a relatively short time.

In cases that do involve disputes, a corresponding number of court sessions will likely be necessary even with trials by lay judges. As to how such court proceedings are carried out, I will discuss this in detail later.

Today, in more than eighty nations around the world, citizens participate in court trials under one of two general systems.

Under the jury system, jury members are responsible for finding the facts in a case, while sentencing is decided by a judge or judges. Jury members are selected to serve for one case only. This system is used in locations including the United States, the British Commonwealth nations, Russia, Spain, Mexico, Brazil, Nicaragua, and Hong Kong.

Under the judge-jury system, judges and laymen pass judgments together. Citizens are appointed to serve for specific periods of time, during which they handle multiple cases. This type of system is currently adopted in Germany, France, Italy, the Scandinavian countries, Africa, and Argentina, among others.

It may be noted that Japan at one time also conducted trials by jury. Based on a law enacted in 1923, trials by a twelve-member jury were carried out starting in 1928. Although the system fell short in various ways—selection for jury duty was limited to males who paid more than three yen in direct national taxes and judges were not bound to decisions rendered by the jury—it was actually implemented for a total of 484 cases, until it was terminated during World War II.

The lay judge trial system newly implemented in Japan resembles the jury system insofar as lay judges are limited to handling one case only; but from the standpoint that lay judges render judgments together with judges, the new system is more akin to the judge-jury system.

Significance of Trials by Lay Judges

According to surveys conducted by the media prior to the start of the lay judge trial system, although many respondents voiced their reluctance to serve as a lay judge, a substantial majority, sixty-five percent, said they would nevertheless probably serve if requested. Combined with the percentage of respondents who expressed interest in serving, the total of willing citizens is thus fairly high.

Overseas also, many people seem reluctant to serve as jury members, and in some countries only about half of those called for jury duty actually appear for screening. Many probably question why they should have to be called up because of some stranger when they themselves are so busy.

Various opinions have been voiced in various quarters about Japan's introduction of the lay judge system. Some say the system is not geared for Japanese people, while others express outright opposition.

Suggestions that the system is not suited to the Japanese or claims that it cannot be implemented successfully in Japan would seem unfounded, however, given how trials by jury were competently carried out in this country during the Showa era before World War II and the long history of trials by jury or judge-jury in locations worldwide. The Japanese are not a "special people" different from everyone else. Why should one think that what has been carried out in so many countries around the world over many years should not be possible in Japan?

In Japan, there are Committees for the Inquest of Prosecution, where deliberations are held concerning cases in which the prosecution filed no indictments. The committees determine whether the prosecution's decision was correct or whether an indictment should be handed down after all. Each committee is made up of eleven members drawn from the general public who serve for a period of six months. Although the system has operated continuously since the end of World War II and more than five hundred thousand Japanese citizens have served on a committee, the existence of the system itself was not widely known—not until the committee chose to override the decision of Tokyo prosecutors not to prosecute Ichiro Ozawa for violation of campaign finance laws. Also, owing to committee members' obligation to maintain total secrecy, there are no opportunities for those who have served under the system to discuss the functioning of the committees.

Surveys of individuals who have served on these inquest committees reveal that, although prior to their service a majority voiced reluctance, once their tenure of service has been completed, ninety-seven to ninety-eight percent of all respondents indicated they were glad to have served.

The Japanese are in general a very serious people. If anything, they are perhaps too serious, which may be taken as a fault. With the lay judge system too, those who end up serving can be expected to perform their duties to the very best of their abilities.

People voice concern that judging others is a difficult affair—an affair, they contend, that would best be left to experts. "Isn't that why we have professional judges?" they say. "Or prosecutors and defense lawyers—isn't that their jobs, too? Let the three of them handle such matters. Don't make us get involved. Don't place the burden on us."

But, are trials really so difficult?

As I stated at the outset, the fundamental role of lay judges is to judge whether or not, in the light of common sense, one can admit, based on the evidence provided, the facts that the prosecution is contending. This process, the admission of facts, is not something that requires any professional prowess; it can be performed adequately just by rendering a judgment based on common sense.

Many countries around the world adopt a jury system. Under the jury system, although professional judges deal with interpreting the law, they do not take part in the process of fact-finding. This is performed solely by the members of the jury. That such a system has continued over a long period suggests that even citizens with no special legal knowledge are fully capable of handling the task of finding the facts in a trial setting.

In Japan, although citizens on occasion participate as members of mediation or judiciary committees in the realm of civil law, they have never done so in the criminal realm—at least not in the postwar era. However, in view of the fact that citizens actually participate and work in the areas of lawmaking and administration, their entry into the criminal realm can be expected to bring transparency to judicial matters—matters that have been left to the "higher-ups" until now—which, as a result, should protect their freedoms and rights all the more.

Opinions and stances on this are likely to differ from person to person. Some probably believe that matters of the sort should best be left to the higher-ups. Others, though, may feel that it would be better if they participated and made decisions together with the higher-ups.

Personally, I think it is precisely in this respect that there is significant meaning in launching the new lay judge trial system.

In an overwhelming majority of instances, the people who have served as professional judges are, generally speaking, people who got good grades in elementary, middle and high school, got into a good university, passed the bar exam without great difficulty, entered the Legal Training and Research Institute, proceeded to get a court job immediately after graduation, and then became a judge and stayed in that position. There are also judges who were former lawyers, but such cases are extremely rare.

People of this ilk have remained professional judges twenty-four hours a day, 365 days a year. These are the people who have consistently presided over the nation's trials.

When a crime of some sort occurs, the police investigate and record their findings in various ways. They may call in people as parties accused of or witnesses to the crime, or they may make arrests, conduct interrogations, or prepare statements. In addition, they conduct investigations of various kinds, such as examining the crime scene, weighing evidence, investigating telephone records, etc. Prosecutors undertake investigations, too. In this way, the nation's investigating agencies compile their investigative records, and based on those records indictments are filed. Should a case be disputed, however, matters do not go along so smoothly.

This is true even with witnesses, for example. If a witness refutes the scenario offered up by the investigators and refuses to sign a statement, his interrogation goes on and on without end. Day in and day out he is told, over and over again, to show up for more investigating. In the Recruit case, dozens of witnesses were called in and questioned for months at a time.

In cases where the accused himself is arrested, the prosecutors are relentless. "Sign this statement!" they will rant. "If you don't, it'll work against you, you know. You'll never get out of detention—and you'll just keep commuting between the detention center and the courthouse." This goes on endlessly. Then, finally, the accused gives in and signs a statement in line with the investigators' scenario. In many instances, when the accused is subjected to a harsh interrogation, it does not take very long before he becomes willing to go along with the story written by the investigators, contrary to the facts though it may be, and signs. All the more so when he is continuously browbeaten and told that he will get out of detention if he admits what the statement says but will stay put where he is if he does not. Nearly everyone placed in such circumstances admits to the charges filed against him.

The fact of the matter is that in nearly all cases the accused party is not released on bail unless he signs the statements placed in front of him. This is why the present trial system is often lambasted as "justice by hostage-taking."

Statements, it might be pointed out, are written not by the individual who is being investigated but by the prosecutors or police officers who conduct the investigation. The person being investigated merely signs his name, and affixes his seal, to confirm that what the statement says is true.

From the standpoint of the person being investigated, the result is a sense of resignation. "What else can I do? I have no choice but to go along with what they're saying. When I get in the courtroom and tell the real truth, the judges will understand. They have to—that's what trials are for."

At least that is what most people assume. In fact, though, the courtroom is not a place where the accused's side of the story is easily acknowledged. In situations where dispute exists, statements are sought to serve as evidence. And in many instances, the point being disputed is none other than whether or not to allow the statements to serve as evidence, or whether or not what the statements say is true.

In court, the prosecuting officers or police officers testify that the accused did indeed say what is written in the statements. "I wrote down precisely what he told me," they declare. The accused, however, refutes this: "It's not that way at all. They forced me to agree to what the statement says. I had no intention of signing it but ultimately I had no alternative."

Exchanges of this sort go on repeatedly, and in cases of this kind what the judge typically does is to assume that what the accused is saying in court is a lie, a willful attempt to make up excuses. Judges take for granted that prosecutors and police officers do not lie. They probably think that since the statements prepared by the investigators are well thought out and logically convincing, the investigators must have done their job thoroughly before writing them up—and therefore the statements are to be believed.

It is physically impossible for a judge to read in court all of the huge number of statements—a veritable mountain of documents—relating to a case. Accordingly, he reads them in his chamber when court is not in session or takes them home and examines them there. Materials of various kinds are submitted not just by the prosecuting side of course, but by the defense as well, so the judge must take all of those documents into consideration as well. He also needs to pore over the records of everything that has transpired in the courtroom.

Judges thus are not judges only while they are in the courtroom; they are on the job as judges all the time, even outside the courtroom. If anything, it is fair to say that the bulk of the work involved related to a ruling is effectively performed outside the courtroom. Judges therefore make their judgments based on what they read in statements outside the courtroom. Attorneys refer to this as "trial by statement."

There is a tendency for judges to conduct fact-finding using patterns: if a fact is established to a certain extent, then the judges find such-and-such to be true. They also tend to trust prosecutors and police officers more than the person on trial. In nearly all instances, they admit statements prepared during the investigative phase as evidence, and they hand down rulings in line with their content.

In very many instances, moreover, the rulings they hand down are written in the same manner: namely, they state that the accused claims such-and-such, but a different such-and-such is also conceivable, and for that reason what the prosecution says is correct. Here again, this is a manifestation of the greater trust placed by judges in the prosecutors. In a nutshell, based on my perception of what takes place, no matter what the accused says, judges generally do not listen with an open mind.

Inherently, a trial should be expected to undertake a thorough check of the investigation carried out by the investigating authorities. If a ruling could be handed down without such checking, then the outcome would be practically set once the investigation ended—and all that would remain would be to send the accused to prison without further ado. A situation of this sort would make trials meaningless and unnecessary. Nevertheless, in an overwhelming number of cases the trial consists simply of confirming the results of the investigating authority's "findings."

Extremely odd though it might be, this state of affairs has continued in Japan's criminal trial system for decades.

Soredemo boku wa yattenai (English title: "I Just Didn't Do It"), a 2007 film directed by Masayuki Suo, is the story of a young man mistakenly accused of groping a woman on a train. The film was notable for its realistic depiction of the criminal trial process in Japan, which was a revelation for viewers—because unless someone is personally involved in a criminal case in some way, he would have no understanding of how the process is carried out.

The nation's bar associations and attorneys have engaged in an array of activities in a quest to break through this deadlocked situation and change the way statements and the like are adopted as evidence. Unfortunately, up until now they have been able to change almost nothing.

Tomorrow, it could be me. You never know when you might find himself under arrest for some reason. There is no way of knowing when you, or an acquaintance, or a friend, or a relative might somehow, somewhere, get entangled in a criminal case. In an extreme scenario, it is possible you will be taken in for a crime of which you are altogether innocent. The type of trial you select may depend on your values.

A fair number of people would probably not wish to be judged by amateurs who have no legal knowledge. Personally, however, I would not want to be put through a trial conducted by judges alone. At trials where virtually nothing that the accused contends will get admitted, those who deserve to be acquitted are not.

Lay judges can be involved in a trial only during a limited period of time, and they are unable to take documents home and examine them in meticulous detail from morning to night. With the introduction of the lay judge system, it is no longer feasible to have mountains of statements pile up to be read and mulled over outside the courtroom. Under these circumstances, while statements will not become meaningless, they will no longer carry the weight as the basis for making judgments.

Lay judges—that is, ordinary citizens—will make judgments based on what they see with their own eyes, examining actual evidence, and hear with their own ears, listening to testimony in court. When statements do get used, they will be read out loud to the lay judges in their entirety. Judgment will then be rendered. The entire contest will be played out and decided in the courtroom.

This is how trials involving citizens' participation will have to be conducted, and I think it could be a significant moment where the status quo of "trials by statement" is changed. Trials by lay judges will bring together people with varied experience, people of varied character and thought. Six persons, each distinctly individual, will join the three judges—a homogeneous trio of professionals who resemble one another and have the same mind-set—in deliberating the cases before them.

Numerous mock trials have been conducted, and numerous attempts at going about deliberations have been tested. From what I have myself seen, the professional judges have been unsure what and how to explain to the lay judges—a situation that quickly descends into a state of confusion. I find this a matter of grave concern. Until now, judgments have been handed down, as I've said, by three professionals who think alike. Although cases come in wide variety, in nearly all instances, even when a fair amount of time has been spent by the three judges in consultation, decisions have likely been reached after rather straightforward discussion. But with the introduction of six laypersons who do not think alike, explanations will now be requested of matters that have previously been treated as apparent and obvious, making it necessary to render judgments while debating such issues in detail. Clearly this will be an extremely taxing process as far as the judges are concerned, but the outcome can be expected to be a considerable change in the way things are conceived and approached.

Citizens who are selected to serve will, of course, come to shoulder a hefty burden. Those with jobs will have to take time off, and participation in a trial itself will unquestionably present a mental burden. All the same, unless citizens enter the picture and change the face of criminal trials as a whole, Japan's criminal trial system will forever remain in the same unsavory state it has long been in.

How the Lay Judge System Works

What changes, specifically, will the lay judge system bring about?

Pre-trial Procedures

Pre-trial procedures refer to the preparations undertaken between the time an indictment is filed and the time the case actually opens in court.

The first step consists of disclosure of evidence by the prosecution to the defense. Under the system that has been in place, rules applied to evidence disclosure have been extremely limited. In trials, evidence which the prosecution intended to introduce in court has had to be shown in advance, but other evidence did not need to be shown to the defense. Even if the defense sought disclosure of such evidence, getting its request fulfilled has proved a challenge. This evidence has ultimately appeared only as the trial played out in the courtroom.

Once the court was actually in session, the prosecution successively introduced each piece of evidence it had earlier requested. If the defense opposed using a statement as evidence, the witness who had signed the statement was asked to testify. The next witness appeared several days or perhaps a month later, causing the trial to go forward in dribs and drabs. This painfully slow, piecemeal way of presenting evidence was very disadvantageous to the defense, which was forced to play things by ear, as it were, as the trial went along.

On occasion important evidence did not appear until the tail end of the proceedings, and sometimes it was not presented at all. In the "Fukawa case"—a murder-robbery that took place in 1967, where the two defendants received life sentences—it was only in the retrial that got under way recently that pieces of important evidence were finally presented in court. In Japan, the evidence disclosure system has been extremely flawed.

Under the latest reforms to the justice system, disclosure of evidence across a broader range is now regulated by law. Although the system is still inadequate in that it does not call for total disclosure, the volume of evidence that must now be disclosed has increased significantly, and as a result, from the outset the defense is better able to grasp just what evidence exists and can form a strategy and tactics in advance.

One reason why trials until now have taken so long is because, since the points in dispute have not been determined ahead of time, the prosecution, having hypothesized various scenarios, seeks to establish the facts across as broad a spectrum as possible, with the result that it presents large volumes of evidence and establishes many facts that have no relation to the final issues in dispute.

Even when the defense requests clarification of detailed facts relating to the indictments or opening arguments by the prosecution, the prosecution is never forthcoming. Meanwhile the defense side, too, does not show its hand until the prosecution has finished its establishment of facts. The effect of all this posturing is that even evidence that is not important to the case has been subjected to thorough examination nonetheless.

The newly introduced pre-trial procedures are aimed at eliminating such wasteful time and effort as much as possible. Simultaneous with the disclosure of evidence by the prosecution, the facts it intends to prove are also made clear. First, the prosecution now submits that a particular fact, by virtue of its being linked to such-and-such evidence, is thus proven. Until now, it was never entirely clear what facts the prosecution would seek to establish using what evidence, but this obfuscation is no longer possible. The defense can now understand clearly, prior to trial, what facts the prosecution will aim to prove using which evidence. As a result, the preparation necessary to build a defense is narrowed down from the outset.

Previously, as a trial moved forward, the claims the prosecution sought to prove occasionally changed midway. If and when the prosecution believed that proving its contention was difficult based on the content of a witness examination, for example, it would change its claims, present new evidence, and conduct a supplementary investigation. Now changes in the prosecution's scheduled establishment of facts will be limited considerably. In this way, after the content of the prosecution's claims and facts to be proven are made clear, the defense will then respond with its own contentions as to where the real facts lie. Prior to the start of court proceedings, the points of dispute will be laid out, the evidence disclosed, and only the necessary evidence will be examined. The aim behind introducing these procedures is to eliminate the superfluous and to concentrate on the necessary.

In the past, with straightforward cases, pre-trial procedures have typically been completed in a short time, but with cases involving serious crime a considerable amount of time has been expended. As an example, in the trial of the person suspected of murdering nine-year-old Goken Yoneyama in Akita in 2006, pre-trial procedures took roughly a year, but there have been cases where pre-trial procedures took more than a year and a half. Now the trend is moving toward disclosing much more evidence than spending time to work out the points of dispute and related evidence, and then focusing the trial only on the critical concerns.

In trials by lay judges, the evidence to be actually examined in court and the points to be argued will be narrowed down prior to the start of the trial. Thus the number of days actually required to conduct court proceedings will be extremely few.

Only after the pre-trial procedures have been completed, the estimated number of days required for the trial worked out, the schedule for court proceedings prepared, and decisions made on who to call as witnesses—in other words, only once all preparations have been completed to allow the trial to begin—will the courts send out notices to candidate lay judges.

Court proceedings will in most cases take fewer days than the trials themselves, usually finishing after two or three days depending on the nature of the case; but in some cases court sessions will continue for two or three weeks. This will depend on how the system is operated going forward.

Selection of Lay Judges

In late November 2008 the Supreme Court sent notices to 290,000 of the nation's citizens informing them that their names had been placed on lists of candidates to serve as lay judges in 2009. Candidates are selected by a draw of lots representing all citizens on voter registration lists, and as such the possibility exists that notifications could go even to people beyond the age of 100. This procedure is to be carried out once every year, and people who have been notified that they have been chosen as a potential lay judge face the possibility of being called sometime in the next year to serve as a lay judge. People who do not receive such notification will not be called.

These potential lay judges are sent a questionnaire. Lawmakers, lawyers, judges, police officers, and civil servants, among others in specified professions, are ineligible to serve as lay judges, and the questionnaire is used to determine whether the recipient falls into any of those categories. The questionnaire also asks whether the recipient is over the age of seventy, is sick or injured, is needed to care for a family member, is scheduled to give birth, etc., and anyone who fits such a description has the option of declining to serve. According to media reports, of the 290,000 notices sent out in November 2008, approximately 70,000 had due cause for declining.

Once a trial is set to begin, notices are sent to several dozen eligible candidates. Normally, notices are sent out six to eight weeks prior to the appointed date of service. Here again, a questionnaire is included, and if a candidate indicates that the time frame specified is inconvenient, the candidate may on occasion be released from the call to service.

Several dozen candidates to be lay judges are actually called for a specified case, but they are not informed of the nature of case until they arrive the courthouse. In prefectures where the number of applicable cases is relatively few, the possibility exists that candidates will know which case they are being called for, given the timing. Basically, however, the candidates do not know in advance anything about the case they will be involved in.

There will be occasions when a candidate will go to the courthouse and discover that the victim is, for example, a personal friend or a former colleague. In such cases the candidate is removed from the list of potential lay judges.

Following the foregoing procedures, ultimately six lay judges are selected per case, augmented by a number of backup candidates. These supplementary lay judges are included in order to be prepared for unforeseen situations such as a lay judge suddenly becoming ill during the trial or, say, a lay judge's wife going into labor. Supplementary lay judges do not participate in deliberations, but they are required to attend the trial through to the handing down of a verdict.

If we assume there will be an estimated three thousand lay judge trials per year, at six lay judges per case this translates to a total of eighteen thousand lay judges; when supplementary judges are added in, this means that in any given year about twenty thousand people nationwide will actually experience service as a lay judge. Over a period of fifty years, this calculates to roughly one million lay judges. The probability of serving as a lay judge would thus not seem to be particularly high.

If anything, there will be more people who go to the courthouse as a lay judge candidate only to be told that their service will not be required and they can return home. Their reporting for potential service will thus have been in vain, but the same holds true for all jury systems around the world. People may think this wastes their time, but it is part of the price one must pay for having such a system. Having citizens participate in criminal trials is important enough to warrant such inconvenience.

Those who are called up as lay judge candidates are paid a per diem of up to eight thousand yen. Those who actually serve as a lay judge receive compensation of up to ten thousand yen a day. Some people might express displeasure at receiving only ten thousand yen for a whole day's time, while others might welcome it as an improvement over a part-time job.

National regulations stipulate how much a trial witness or member of a prosecution inquest panel is paid per day, so the Ministry of Finance likely does not feel it is in a position to offer higher compensation only to lay judges alone. All the same, a per diem of eight thousand or ten thousand yen is fairly high compared to systems in other countries.

The Trial Process

Prior to the start of their assigned trial, the individuals selected to serve as lay judges are given explanations of how a criminal trial plays out and the general rules governing such trials.

Among the points explained to them are that a defendant is presumed innocent until a guilty verdict is handed down; that a defendant is found guilty when, against the yardstick of common sense, the claims sought to be established by the prosecution are confirmed; that a verdict of innocence is handed down when there is doubt surrounding the claims of the prosecution; and that the defendant has the right to remain silent and is thus at liberty to say nothing at all during his trial. After these explanations have been completed, the trial is ready to commence.

First, the defendant is asked to state his name, address, legal domicile, date of birth, and occupation. The prosecution then reads the indictments in the case. The presiding judge informs the defendant of his right to remain silent, after which the defendant states his opinion concerning the indictments. The defense attorney does likewise.

Next, the prosecution and defense respectively present their opening statements. In trials previously, in nearly all instances no such statement has been made by the defense; under the lay judge trial system, however, the defense side must also offer up an opening statement to the court.

With cases involving serious crimes, the opening remarks by the prosecution are at times reported by the media, and frequently such reports are worded in such a way as to suggest that the outcome is a given. In other words, they give the impression that once the prosecution has delivered its opening statement the case against the defendant is a foregone conclusion.

Japan's conviction rate of 99.8 percent. In virtually all cases, the records of the investigation are confirmed as they appear, the outcome essentially set in stone. To put it bluntly, once you're indicted, you're as good as guilty.

Prosecutors have the discretion to decide whether or not to issue an indictment, and apparently they think that since they indict someone only in cases when they believe that the individual is definitely guilty, it is only natural for the conviction rate to be 99.8 percent.

Of the eighty to ninety thousand criminal cases recorded every year, however, in a fairly large number—five to six thousand—the accused denies guilt.

A denial of guilt is not limited to instances when a defendant contends he is totally innocent; in cases of murder, a denial may include the defendant's contention that he had no intent to kill. All the same, of the five to six thousand cases where a defendant denies the charge against him, an innocent verdict is handed down in only about one hundred. A few years ago, the number was even smaller: between fifty and sixty per year.

For there to be only one hundred or so acquittals among five to six thousand claims of denial must be said to be unnatural—and uncanny. I speak from experience when I say there have been many cases where, no matter how thoroughly and effectively the defense has argued to prove the client's innocence, the defendant's claims are rejected.

The opening statement made in court by the prosecution is no more than the prosecutors' construction of the scenario they will attempt to prove. By the same token, the opening remarks by the defense are no more than the defense's argument that the case in truth has quite a different scenario.

Consider this hypothesis: what would be the verdict if it were handed down at this stage, before the evidence is examined? The answer is simple: the defendant would have to be found innocent. This is because the contentions made by the prosecution are just that: contentions. At this stage neither has any evidence been presented; nor has anything been proven. Only when evidence exists and the prosecution's side of the story is admitted can a guilty verdict be passed. This is the rule a presumption of innocence until proven guilty.

The current trend, concluding that a defendant must be guilty based on the prosecution's opening argument alone, is not only odd in the extreme, it is contrary to judicial principle.

Once the opening statements are completed, the trial proceeds into detailed questioning of witnesses and examination of evidence.

Witnesses called by the prosecution are initially questioned by the prosecutor, a process referred to as direct examination. The defense then cross-examines the witness, attacking what it sees to be contradictions in testimony, pointing out objective inconsistencies with the facts of the case, or indicating how the witness's position or situation slants his testimony, all in a quest to ferret out reasons why the testimony is unreliable. In real life, only rarely do such cross-examinations take on the dramatic aura typically featured in films or television. What does occur with relative frequency is the cross-examiner points out differences between what a witness had said prior to the trial and what he is now saying in court. As to which story falls in line with the facts, this is judged according to the situations in which the two versions had been stated.

If evidence has been submitted in the form of a written document, the prosecution reads it aloud. The lay judges listen to grasp what is being offered as evidence. The document itself, having been submitted to the court, is available for subsequent review.

When evidence contains drawings or photographs, the drawings or photographs are shown in the courtroom. Monitors are set up inside the courtroom—a small one in front of the lay judges and a large one for viewing by visitors seated in the gallery.

When evidence consists of a knife or other weapon used in the crime, the actual item is presented in the courtroom.

Recently, computer graphics are sometimes used, but this differs from actual evidence. In many instances computer graphics are used, for example, to convey simply the original evidence in the form of a written opinion by an expert or to recreate the circumstances under which the crime took place. Since the "facts" thus presented are claims made by the party involved in the case and *not* evidence, lay judges need to exercise caution.

In response to the prosecution's presentation of what it claims to be the facts, the defense calls its witnesses and presents its evidence. The methods used by the defense to question witnesses and examine evidence are identical to those used by the prosecution.

Often, the facts of a case are not disputed. When that happens, the witnesses called by the defense attest to the defendant's upbringing, personality, and circumstances behind the crime. These witnesses tend to be the defendant's employer, relatives, senior colleagues, and so forth. At times the defendant will speak on his own behalf, pointing out circumstances advantageous to his position.

Recently, in addition to the foregoing, on occasion the victim, members of a deceased victim's family, or the attorney representing them will sit next to the prosecution in court and question witnesses concerning circumstances or the defendant concerning the crime. This innovation has been introduced based on a new system recently launched that permits participation of victims of the crime. Until now, victims have played a passive role, limited to giving testimony as a witness or stating their views in court. Now, they can also pose questions to witnesses or to the defendant, and they are also permitted to state their opinion on sentencing.

This system was implemented to address the sense that the concerns of the victim had not been adequately reflected in criminal trials. For the defense attorney, however, the effect of this implementation is that there is another party of interest that must now be dealt with. If the defense attorney has prepared defense strategy thoroughly, though, the system does not work to any particular disadvantage.

After the examination of evidence has been completed, the prosecution presents its closing argument and asks for a specific sentence. The prosecutor states that the facts claimed by the prosecution have been corroborated based on the evidence as examined, and it asks for what it suggests is the appropriate prison sentence.

In response, the defense pleads its case, but in trials until now the arguments presented by both the prosecution and the defense have been limited to written texts which the two sides would respectively read aloud in court. The judges listened as these texts were read, but with major cases such texts could run to book length. These were thus read out at brisk speed, on occasion abbreviating for convenience, making it impossible for the listener to understand their full content. Judges would later reread these closing arguments, and when examining the evidence they would sit on a ruling while checking the texts where necessary. In all instances, the outcome was mulled over based on the written word.

Lay judges do not read such lengthy arguments after arguments have been made, nor can they be asked to do so. For this reason, the arguments presented by both the prosecution and the defense have to be easily understandable, both aurally and visually, within the courtroom. Reading long texts aloud cannot win lay judges' comprehension—or favor.

With sentencing also, the defense now must respond in a different way from what had been done previously. Until now the prosecution asked for a specific sentence, that is, such-and-such number of years in prison, and the defense responded merely that a suspended sentence is warranted, that the death sentence is inappropriate and incarceration for life should suffice, etc. In almost no instances did the defense take its response one step further to suggest a specific number of years as a more appropriate sentence.

Going forward, however, there are likely to be more occasions when the defense will respond to the prosecution's call for sentencing and state its own view on sentencing. Given how the victim's side will also be indicating in specific terms its view on sentencing, the need for the defense to do likewise will be all the greater. The defense is now called upon to indicate a specific sentence and to explain its reasoning and underlying basis in a manner that will make it easy for the lay judges to render their judgment.

Currently the courts are preparing a database on sentencing. Such a database had already been in the making, but since April 2008 data relating to cases applicable to the lay judge trial system is being input in an array of categories: for example, the number of victims and level of damage sustained in each case, how the crime was committed, the objects used in committing the crime, the defendant's previous criminal record, etc. Using this information, graphs and tables are to be prepared. These materials will be made available to the lay judges during their deliberations, enabling them to get an overview of sentencing trends in similar cases.

Because the same data can be used by both the prosecution and the defense, it will be possible for both sides to make reference to such information in their closing arguments.

Deliberation, Verdict, and Ruling

Once all court proceedings have been completed, the six lay judges and three court judges begin their joint deliberations. Such deliberations are not carried out exclusively after the trial proceedings, however; during the trial itself, lay judges and court judges may, when necessary, exchange opinions and discuss their impressions with one another.

In their deliberations, conducted in a chamber set aside for this purpose, the nine members deliberate on the particulars of the case, and although the court judges are the legal specialists here, the lay judges must not feel any constraint about speaking up. The aims of the lay judge system itself call for lay judges to ask as many questions as they wish, no matter how rudimentary, and to express their views freely.

Indeed, the Act Concerning Participation of Lay Judges in Criminal Trials stipulates that the presiding judge must pay heed to enable the lay judges to carry out their assigned duties fully—for example, by taking steps so that the deliberations will be readily understandable to the lay judges, creating sufficient opportunities for the lay judges to express their views, etc.

Based on this Act, the Supreme Court has set down its own rules, and here again it is stipulated that court judges must, in the course of the deliberations, pay heed to ensuring that the lay judges will each express his or her opinion based on the content of the court proceedings and that full exchange of opinions will be carried out among the judging panel's constituent members. Brisk voicing of opinions is thus proactively sought.

In the deliberation process, the votes cast by court judges and lay judges carry exactly the same weight. In reaching their conclusion, a unanimous decision is desirable, and adequate and sustained discussions are required. When the views of all members are not unanimous, stipulations call for a decision ultimately to be rendered based on the majority vote.

In trials by jury, unanimous agreement is a principal requirement, but in the Japanese trial system decisions are fundamentally reached by a majority vote. Cases decided by a panel of three judges in a district court are known as "collegial cases," and in the high courts all cases are collegial. At the Supreme Court level, all cases are decided by a majority vote: among five members in petty bench cases and among fifteen members in full bench cases.

Under the new lay judge trial system also, finding of facts and weighing of the sentence are now determined by a majority vote among the nine judges, both court and lay. In order to pass a guilty verdict, however, both court and lay judges must be included among those members casting the majority vote decision. In other words, the system is set up so that at least one court judge must be included among those who find the defendant guilty.

Many opinions have been voiced concerning decisions on sentencing. Some harbor doubt about the ability of amateurs to make judgments of such importance, while others are apprehensive about a trend toward heavier punishments when lay judges are included in the sentencing process. Are such fears warranted?

How do judges come to their decisions on sentencing? If, for example, the prosecution is asking for a ten-year sentence, when the contentions being made by the prosecution differ somewhat from the actual evidence in the case, the ruling judges typically opt for a sentence somewhat shorter than asked for: in this case, perhaps eight years. The result is a tendency whereby the longer the sentence the prosecution asks for, the heavier will be the sentence meted out by the court.

For a fact, perhaps as a consequence of recent legal revisions where statutory penalties against criminal offenses have been made heavier, prosecutors appear to be asking for increasingly weightier sentences. And in line with that tendency, the rulings passed by judges are also becoming heavier.

To be specific, under revisions to the Criminal Code enacted in 2005, the upper limit on standard non-life sentences was raised from fifteen years to twenty, and when the nature of the crime calls for heavier punishment, the upper limit has been increased from twenty years to thirty. Simultaneously the lower limit for sentences imposed in cases of homicide was raised from three years to five; in cases of injury resulting in death, from two years to three; in cases of rape resulting in death, from three years to five; and in cases of dangerous driving causing death, the upper limit on sentencing was raised from fifteen years to twenty.

Although it would be rash to generalize, based on what I personally have seen in trial simulations, court judges tend to consider heavier sentences than lay judges. Judgments rendered by lay judges span a broad spectrum: some call for extremely heavy sentences while others propose extremely light punishments.

And it is not surprising that this is another point where opinions toward the lay judge system divide. On my own part, I think this absence of uniformity in the opinions of lay judges is favorable. It is hoped that out of such diversity the court and lay judges as a group will come to a consensus in rendering their decisions.

For a defense lawyer as myself, it is necessary to conduct defense activities in such a way that lay judges can gain a full understanding of the actual circumstances surrounding the case at hand. Once that understanding is achieved, next, with respect to sentencing, it is necessary to suggest, citing a specific number of years, what an appropriate sentence would be. One would need to indicate the basis for believing why such-and-such a sentence is appropriate, using a database on previous sentences meted out as well as other materials.

It has been said that when determining the facts of a case and weighing sentencing, lay judges are likely to be influenced by the media. To be quite frank, one has wondered whether professional judges have all along been so completely immune to the media.

To illustrate, at the very first court session in the Recruit trial, where I served on the defense team, when the defense requested explanation of the indictments, the presiding judge let slip his assessment that the issue at hand was the value of the shares involved and whether they constituted profit. The judge made that statement at a stage when examination of the evidence had yet to begin. Could it be that in the Recruit case, in the face of the deluge of media reporting, guilt was already established? The conventional wisdom notwithstanding, professional judges are no less impacted by the media—just like anyone else—and lay judges are not likely to be an exception either.

With attorneys such as myself as well, to follow media reports about cases in which we are not involved—and to assume that everything must be just as being reported—is not uncommon. We do so because we have no other material on which to base our judgments. But if we do become involved in a case, see the evidence for ourselves, and hear actual testimony, we immediately know which parts of what the media has been reporting are factual and which parts are not.

Being influenced by the media is to some extent unavoidable, but I do not think the view that media influence would be especially great just because a lay judge is an ordinary citizen holds water.

One aspect of the lay judge system often criticized is the obligation of lay judges to maintain absolute secrecy.

There does not appear to be any objection to requiring absolute confidentiality while the trial is in progress, and confidentiality seems to be mandatory in all countries that adopt trial systems involving ordinary citizens. Where the concern arises is in the obligation to maintain secrecy even after the trial has ended, as well as in the penalty that would be imposed for any violation of this obligation.

Although people say it would be impossible to keep such secrets all their lives, lay judges can say certain things about what happened in the courtroom without its constituting a violation of confidentiality. For example, just like observers who attend open court sessions, lay judges can describe—without being subject to penalty—what a witness said at such-and-such a point in the trial or relate what kind of evidence was presented. What lay judges are prohibited from discussing are the details of their deliberations, the opinions expressed by the lay judges themselves or by the court judges, and the way the voting went. They are forbidden from leaking any secrets they learned through their judicial duties, as well as their personal assessments of fact-finding during the trial or the sentencing. Generally speaking, they are thus requested not to divulge who said what during the course of the deliberations or their individual views concerning the appropriateness of specific aspects of the trial.

The obligation to maintain secrecy is actually imposed in consideration of the court judges and lay judges, for if the situation allowed any declarations during deliberations to be revealed, this would prevent them from expressing their views freely during the deliberations.

Mandatory confidentiality is also a feature of the British jury system. Any violation of that obligation results in punishment for contempt of court. By contrast, in the United States, where the jury system is also in place, jury members are not obligated to maintain secrecy once the trial closes, and they are free to respond to media questions without penalty. Judges in the United States. do apparently advise jury members to keep quiet, but in that country greater importance seems to be attached to freedom of the press and the right to free speech.

While I do think a confidentiality obligation is necessary to some extent in order to guarantee the realization of free deliberations, I do not think it is appropriate to impose the heavy penalty of up to six months' imprisonment; I take less objection to a fine. This, I think, is a point meriting reform in the future.

Under the lay judge system, the names of lay judges are not made public. As such, in a big city like Tokyo with so many cases coming to trial, who has served as a lay judge in a particular case remains largely unknown. If a company employee submitted a request for time off and had to state a reason, then, perhaps, a small circle would know, but on the whole it would not be common knowledge.

In regions with small populations and only a small number of cases applicable to trial by lay judges, knowing when someone is serving as a lay judge would not be unlikely. In countries adopting the jury system, a person might be born, grew up, and lived his entire life in the same location, and if that person served on a jury, everyone in the community would know. Moreover, given the principle calling for unanimous decisions, it would be clearly known whether a particular person had voted for or against a conviction. Nonetheless, even in such instances, trial by jury is carried out without problem. Depending on the nature of the crime involved, there are occasions when a trial is held at a different location, but this is exceptional.

With trials by lay judges, because decisions are made based on a majority vote and are not unanimous, it cannot be known what was the individual judgment of each lay judge. In this respect, so long as a certain level of secrecy concerning the deliberations is maintained, how a lay judge votes is unlikely to be made into a local issue.

The greater issue is how society in general reacts to the verdict reached in a particular trial. Will that verdict be acceptable to the local community, and in the event that it is not, how will the local community respond to the individuals who served as lay judges? Once lay judge trials get solidly on track this is something that should not be of great concern, even as the introduction of the lay judge system provides an occasion for once again considering how local societies function.

The opinion has been expressed that a system of participation by citizens in criminal trials is alien to Japanese culture. Because education in Japan does not foster the ability to engage proactively in discussion, critics say, it is futile for lay judges with no trial experience to debate matters with professional judges.

Even in everyday business settings, however, company employees do regularly exchange opinions, so it is hard to imagine that Japanese citizens are incapable of taking part in such discussions. Nor does the argument hold water that the lay judge system is alien to Japan on the vague grounds of the alleged nature of its culture. I would suggest that the only issue with the system is, for now, the lack of familiarity with trials.

The role of lay judges is to decide whether the defendant in a criminal trial is guilty or innocent. Because the Japanese justice system still allows for capital punishment, in some cases therefore lay judges must make a decision whether to impose a death sentence. This, undeniably, will constitute a burden for the lay judge.

But in relation to this, there may be a need to rethink the fact that as Japanese we are living in a society that permits capital punishment and to consider what judgment should be made concerning crimes that are perpetrated within that context. Globally, the trend is toward suspending or eliminating capital punishment. Meanwhile in Japan the number of criminals sentenced to death keeps growing.

It is not my interest here to discuss the rightness or wrongness of this practice. But if, for example, a lay judge feels that the imposition of a death sentence is beyond his or her capacity to do so, this should lead to debate concerning whether a system that permits capital punishment is truly necessary.

Even with concerns of this kind, I feel there is great meaning and benefit in having ordinary citizens directly involved in criminal trials. Such involvement is tantamount to reconsidering and making decisions about the mechanisms of the society in which we live.

Clearly, the new system is fraught with issues. Nevertheless, my hope is that those who are called as candidate lay judges will take up the chance to experience the system for themselves and participate in a real trial. From my position as an attorney, I have high hopes that in contrast to the situation we have had until now when, no matter what we said, judges were unwilling to accept our contentions, now, finally, our contentions will have a chance of being accepted.

The bar associations had sought to bring in a jury system. Some people wanted a joint judge-jury system. The newly adopted lay judge system, a compromise, had not been sought by anyone; yet I sense that it will be a huge improvement from the way criminal trials have been conducted until now.

I would even go so far as to conjecture that many lawyers, for whom criminal trials have conventionally seemed futile affairs, will come to see criminal trials as undertakings in which their efforts will be rewarded. I also think it should be possible to prevent, even to a limited extent, situations in which a defendant is charged with a crime that he never committed.

I see a ray of hope on the horizon.

Reform of the Justice System

Background

In the previous pages I have touched upon how the new lay judge system works and the significance of the new system. Here, I would like to discuss how the system came about and whether changes have been effected to any other aspects of the criminal justice system.

It was not only the criminal justice system that was called into question; the entire justice system was ripe for overhaul, a process that got under way in 1999. In the run-up to the twenty-first century, reforms were being implemented in various areas—in the political and administrative arenas, in government decentralization, and in restructuring the economy through deregulation. This overall trend has been referred to as a metamorphosis from an "advanced-control" society to a "post-check" society. Targets included disclosure of information and complete accountability to citizens, extrication from government functioning as big brother, and a transition to citizens taking a central role in governing.

Justice system reforms aimed to link these various reforms under the constitutional doctrine of "rule of law." In July 1999 the Justice System Reform Council was established within the Cabinet.

Although the council members, thirteen in all, included people in the legal profession, in number they were limited to only one scholar of criminal law and three practicing attorneys at law, including one former judge and one former prosecutor. The remaining members were corporate managers, an author, and a labor union official. Experts in criminal justice were thus in the minority, and it is this roster of members that apparently enabled the council to separate itself from the entanglements of the justice system and to propose bold reforms.

The council met on sixty-three occasions, the last being in June 2001, and during this time members held hearings around the country and visited courts, probation offices, and other venues. On June 12, 2001, they released their findings in "Recommendations of the Justice System Reform Council—For a Justice System to Support Japan in the 21st Century."

Recommendations spanned the gamut of the justice system, including calls for reform of the civil justice system, reform of the criminal justice system, responses to internationalization, expansion of the legal population, reform of the legal training system, reform of the lawyer system, reform of the public prosecutor system, reform of the judge system, . . . The council then proposed introducing the lay judge system as a way of getting citizens to participate in the administration of justice.

It was based on the council's recommendations that the number of successful bar exam examinees is now increasing sharply and that a new legal training system—law schools—was launched. These developments have engendered a major transformation in the core mechanisms of the justice system long entrenched during the postwar era. The new system aims to realize a highly transparent society in which legal resolutions can be sought in every aspect and at every level, and to implement the system large numbers of jurists are to be trained. At the same time, the system is targeted at strengthening the base that underpins the administration of justice through the participation of ordinary citizens.

Based on the council's recommendations, experts in criminal law, criminal justice administrators, media representatives, and social pundits met at the Office for Promotion of Justice System Reform to discuss the lay judge and criminal justice systems. As a result of those meetings, the Act Concerning Participation of Lay Judges in Criminal Trials was enacted in May 2004.

It was also out of those deliberations that the new system of pre-trial procedures, noted earlier in discussing how lay judge trials work, was born.

The Remaining Task: Bringing Visibility to Interrogations

The council's achievements aside, reforms to rectify various problems in the justice system were not realized because of a failure to reach a consensus. Such issues still need to be addressed, and one of the most critical among them is the matter of bringing visibility to interrogations.

Recently this issue of recording interrogations of crime suspects, both sound and video, has finally begun to be taken up by the media.

Any time a person is arrested on suspicion of having committed a crime or called in as a witness, he or she undergoes questioning in an interrogation room at the police station or public prosecutors office. At a police station, interrogations are conducted by several police officers, while at a public prosecutors office questioning takes place in the presence of a prosecutor and an assistant officer charged with the clerical work. The person under interrogation is on his own: the presence of his or her own lawyer is not permitted.

The results of the interrogation are compiled into documents known as a statement. It is not the person being interrogated who prepares the statement, however, but rather the interrogating police officer or prosecutor. Only rarely does the statement take the form of a record of each question asked of the interrogated individual and his responses. Instead, it is drawn up as though the interrogated party were writing down his own words; for example: "On such-and-such date I went to such-and-such place, met with so-and-so, and we talked about such-and-such."

At the end of the statement, the suspect signs his name and affixes his seal, after which a sentence is added to the effect that the interrogator—either the police officer or prosecutor—had read the foregoing recorded statement to the suspect and that the suspect had confirmed that it

contained no errors and signed his name and affixed his seal. That com-
ment in turn is signed and seal-affixed by the interrogating police officer or
prosecutor. Once the two signatures and seals are added to the statement,
its content is considered correct.

There have been cases of false accusation, however, in which, despite the
suspect's signature and seal at the end of his statement, it subsequently has
come to light that the content of the statement was not factual. Moreover,
even in cases that could not be called instances of false accusation, because
it is the interrogating officer who prepares the statement and not the suspect himself, it often happens that what is written in it is not what the
suspect actually said; the assumptions and contentions of the interrogating
officer, though different from the accused's intent, are written as though
they had been spoken by the accused.

The result is that during the ensuing trial, conflicts occur concerning the
content of statements, as noted above. It is to eliminate such conflicts that
current efforts to introduce full video recording of interrogations, from
start to finish, are being made.

The police and public prosecutors oppose such a move.

Today, in certain cases, after a suspect has confessed, a video recording—usually twenty to thirty minutes in length—is made at the police station or public prosecutors office. Bar associations are against this, however,
on the grounds that unless a video record is made not partially but of the
entire interrogation process, it is impossible to scrutinize the content of the
interrogation. They say that partial recording is not only meaningless but
actually makes it difficult to examine whether the suspect had earlier been
subjected to bargaining, promise of special treatment or threats, forcing
him to make a false confession against his will.

In voicing their opposition to full video recording, police officials and
public prosecutors cite several reasons. Among them, they point out that in
order to build a relationship of trust with a suspect and get him to open up
and divulge what really happened, during their interrogations they often
confidentially reveal their own private affairs—something, they claim, they

could not do completely if everything were being videoed. Also, they contend that in cases of organized crime, if as a result of video recording the organization came to know which of its members had said what, a suspect's life would clearly be put at risk.

As a matter of fact, on one occasion the police did record its interrogations, and there have been instances when such recordings were used, in part, during the course of the subsequent trial. So the police recorded when they found doing so helpful to their purposes, and in some cases they succeeded in drawing out a confession. In those instances, the police and public prosecutors contended that such confessions were truthful. Of course, this directly contradicts the claim that the truth will not come out if interrogations are recorded.

If confessions are made on the foundation of a relationship of trust, then why do we sometimes find such confessions thrown out during the trial? They get jettisoned because they were not built on a relationship of any trust in the true sense. At the most fundamental level, given the overwhelming gap between their respective positions, there is probably no such thing as a relationship of "trust" between an interrogator and the person being interrogated. And it is the "relationship" forged behind closed doors that creates a situation ripe for false confessions. The ability to examine what had taken place within those confines is critical.

Under the situation as it now stands, statements are drawn up in any number and they all get used as evidence, even in cases involving organized crime. The reservations made by the police and public prosecutors thus are exceptional. Granted, with cases involving organized crime there may be instances when someone might talk but ask not to have what he reveals drawn up in a statement. There is no way of knowing, however, whether or not what he says during the interrogation is actually true. He may be making his whole story up in order to foist blame for the crime on someone else. Even if what the interrogated party says is true, that is no reason not to make a recording of his interrogation. Outside Japan, cases of this nature are resolved by addressing the question of how to protect such a witness. Telling the truth does not qualify as a reason for not making a record.

What then is the situation regarding video and sound recording outside Japan?

In England, full sound recording of interrogations has been mandatory since 1992, and since 2002 full video recording is being carried out on a trial basis. Sound recording of interrogations is said to have resulted in substantial advances in interrogation techniques. Police authorities have developed new interrogatory skills, and those skills are being taught to police officers.

In Australia, full sound and video recordings are made of interrogations, with slight variations from state to state. Their adoption has reduced dissatisfaction toward police interrogations, and rather than leading to fewer confessions, full recording has actually boosted the number of guilty pleas. Police authorities thus welcome recording of their interrogations.

In the United States, attorneys are permitted to sit in on interrogations. Nonetheless, the number of states where interrogations of detained suspects are recorded in total is increasing. Many police agencies approve of video and sound recording.

In Canada, rulings have been handed down by provincial superior courts that reject the voluntariness of a confession on the grounds that no sound or video recording was made at the time.

In Italy, statements for which no sound or video recording exists cannot be used as evidence in court.

In France, full video recording of police interrogations has been mandatory since June 2008.

In Hong Kong, a suspect being interrogated by the police has the right to request full video and sound recording of the interrogation.

In Taiwan, a system mandating full video and sound recording of interrogations was codified in 1998.

In Korea, when a statement prepared by a police officer is disputed, it cannot be used as evidence unless its content is proved using a video record. Full video and sound recording is spreading among police authorities.

In Mongolia, investigating authorities are permitted to make video recordings. Attorney requests for video recording are increasing.

In China, full video recording was launched on a trial basis in March 2006 in cases involving corruption by a public servant.

Clearly, the trend worldwide is moving toward full video and sound recording of investigations and interrogations.

In Japan too, the Democratic Party of Japan has repeatedly submitted a bill calling for mandatory full video and sound recording of interrogations, but as yet passage has proved elusive. With the change of administration, however, the likelihood of the bill's passage has improved. Even now the police authorities and public prosecutors are vehemently opposed to full video recording, but the tide is moving with alacrity toward bringing visibility to interrogations. Once that tide comes to shore, one of the major issues remaining in the justice system reform agenda will be resolved.

In the newly launched lay judge trials also, we see occasions when the content of statements made during interrogations is repeatedly confirmed in the courtroom. Issues of this nature will be resolved simply if interrogations are made visible; any time there is a discrepancy between a statement made in court and a statement made during the corresponding interrogation, the matter can be fully examined during the pre-trial procedures, and the whole issue can be resolved by confirming the recording of the pertinent scene in the courtroom.

Today, now that legislation has been set in place, justice system reforms have finally gotten under way. And although in some instances—bringing visibility to interrogations, for example—moves toward legislative enactment are now in motion, all systems will need to be monitored from a long-range perspective. Legal practitioners will need to make ongoing and sustained efforts to put the new systems solidly on track. To do so, clearly it will be indispensable to place the systems under the critical scrutiny of the nation's citizens at all times.

The justice system is meant to serve the people. It is they who should oversee its development.

Masanori Ono. Born in 1948. Graduated from the University of Tokyo, Faculty of Law; passed the bar exam, 1972. Entered Legal Training and Research Institute of Japan, 1973. Became Attorney at Law, registered with the Dai-ni Tokyo Bar Association, 1975. Established Kamiyacho Law & Accounting Office, 1980; reorganized as New Tokyo Law & Accounting Office, 1980; reorganized as Tokyo Liberté, 2001.

As an officer of the Dai-ni Tokyo Bar Association, has served as chairman of the Legal Apprentice Training Committee, Court Committee, and Criminal Defense Committee; as deputy chairman of the Permanent Members Council, vice chairman of the Dai-ni Tokyo Bar Association. As an officer of the Japan Federation of Bar Associations, has served as vice chairman of the Legal Apprentice Training Committee and Criminal Defense Center, deputy director of the Interrogation Visibility Realization Headquarters, acting director of the Lay Judge Headquarters, and Executive Governor, among other positions.

VI

TRIALS BY LAY JUDGES: START OF A NEW ERA

Etsuyoshi Izuta, Attorney at Law

May 2009 saw the greatly anticipated launch of the lay judge system. The system had long been considered the centerpiece of the justice system reform agenda, and the triumvirate within the legal realm—the nation's courts, public prosecutors offices, and bar associations—had made concerted efforts to promote public awareness of the new system. The first trials conducted under the new system at the various district courts were reported by the media in such great detail, the events almost took on the feeling of live broadcasting.

The reason why attention focused on those first trials to such extent is because the lay judge system marks a radical reform of the nation's traditional criminal justice proceedings. I myself, in my role as an attorney, have been involved in those proceedings for fourteen or fifteen years, and I believe the introduction of the lay judge system will have massive impact on a par with that of the "black ships" that arrived off Japan's shores in the mid-nineteenth century and abruptly forced an end to the archipelago's entrenched isolation.

With the launch of the lay judge system, decisions in criminal trials, until now the exclusive prerogative of professional judges, are now reached with the participation of ordinary citizens. Moreover, in rendering a final judgment based on the criminal trial proceedings, citizens who participate as lay judges are free to express their opinions as an equal with professional judges.

On the positive side, what this signifies is the acquisition by Japanese citizens of the right to participate in criminal trials as a decision maker. But at the same time citizens selected to serve as lay judges must take on extremely weighty responsibility and fulfill a highly demanding role.

Rulings handed down in line with criminal justice proceedings take two principal forms: the finding of facts in the case, which is a ruling as to whether the defendant is guilty or innocent; and, should the defendant be found guilty, the weighing of a sentence, that is, ruling on a punishment to fit the crime. These rulings have a large impact on the lives of numerous people: not only on the defendant, but also family members and others close to the defendant, as well as the victims of the crime and their families (in some cases, bereaved).

Of special note is that cases applicable to the lay judge system may be crimes in which a victim has died as a result of a premeditated act or which may warrant the penalty of death or life imprisonment. In other words, of all the criminal trials conducted in Japan, lay judges will only participate in cases that belong to the category of very serious crimes. Given the significance attached to rulings in such criminal cases, the role assigned to lay judges is literally to decide the fate of a human being. The weight of that responsibility is self-evident, for if lay judges make the wrong decision in a case, the consequences can wreak havoc on many lives.

As an attorney, in overwhelming proportion my role in criminal trial proceedings is to serve on the side of the accused under suspicion or the defendant under prosecution. For that reason, to be quite frank, I am unable, even now that the system is in place, to swallow my slight misgivings about having ordinary citizens with no legal experience whatsoever sit in judgment and hand down a ruling.

Why did the powers that be, knowing full well the gravity of the responsibility they would be placing on the shoulders of ordinary citizens, call for laymen's participation in criminal trial proceedings? The answer might be a quest to inject a dose of sound "common" sense into the nation's criminal trials.

Stating this might invite the misunderstanding that I think that a criminal trial conducted by professional judges alone is unsound; this is by no means my intention. In Japan, criminal justice proceedings have long been referred to as "precision-made justice," owing to the slow and cautious pace of court proceedings, where vast quantities of evidence are examined and analyzed in minute detail—a rigor that has been evaluated quite highly, I might add.

However, perhaps because of the desire to exercise such precision, professional judges have often been viewed as tending toward the rigid and inflexible. This perception grew even as social interaction in Japan became more varied and complex and as society began to embrace more diverse values. Plainly put, doubts were harbored as to whether the sense of professional judges—people whose appointments are, like public servants, made on the premise of lifetime employment, who tread an elite path, and who have few opportunities to experience situations outside the courtroom—coincided with the common sense of ordinary citizens.

Japan's precision-made justice has been sustained by the "confessions" prepared by the investigative agencies after they have completed their interrogations of the accused. No matter how assiduously professional judges might seek to ascertain the facts of a case based on the totality of available evidence, in reality there are too many instances when circumstances cannot be known without a confession by the defendant himself. This is why judges, in their eagerness to maintain precise fact-finding, have tended to rely on these so-called confessions. Within the investigative agencies also, the awareness has been clear that the courts require a confession, and so in order to secure a conviction they have poured all the more effort into securing confessions. This chain of circumstances has had the effect of placing undue pressure on the defendant, creating the risk that an innocent person could be coerced into making a false confession, resulting in the tragic situation of someone falsely accused being punished for a crime he did not commit.

In my position as an attorney, I believe that the significance of the newly introduced lay judge system lies in its sincere intent to rectify the foregoing injustices that have been inherent in the precision-made justice system.

First, the value of injecting a dose of a layman's perspective into criminal trials may be realized in situations where a defendant's contentions cannot easily be understood by professional judges but which, in the light of the common sense of a layman, seem reasonable.

Second, under the lay judge system, the conventional practice of having judges pore over vast quantities of documents, including the defendant's alleged confession, outside the courtroom will no longer be possible. The focus of the in-court proceedings will now be on actual verbal exchanges conducted in the courtroom. (This method of conducting court proceedings, referred to as "direct" or "oral" argument, was adopted under the earlier system, but in real terms had descended to mere formality.) This induces the hope that the contentions of the defendant himself, expressed in his own words directly in the lay judges' presence, might be more convincing than a confession wrenched from him by investigators behind closed doors.

Because of my experience with the Recruit trial as the most junior member of the defense team, I wish here to relate, in no particular order, various events in my relatively brief career that have left a deep impression as regards the lay judge system.

The Recruit Case and the Layman's View

One of the important concepts behind the lay judge system is the layman's perspective. And what invariably comes to mind when I ponder the relationship between criminal trials and this perspective of the layman is the issue surrounding the purchase of a supercomputer as it figured into the Recruit case.

The Recruit case was a case dealing with bribery and therefore it was not a case that would be tried under the new lay judge system. Nevertheless, I have often thought that had ordinary citizens participated in the Recruit trial proceedings, the findings and verdict handed down to Mr. Ezoe would probably have been very different.

Among the various charges filed in the Recruit case, the "NTT route" dealt with allegations concerning the sale of pre-flotation shares to several people at NTT (Nippon Telegraph and Telephone), the former public corporation that was privatized in 1985. One of the points of dispute was the alleged provision of favored treatment from NTT to Recruit involving the purchase of a Cray supercomputer.

At the heart of the issue was Recruit's September 1985 purchase of a supercomputer not from Cray itself but indirectly through NTT. NTT's role fueled suspicions that NTT extended this favor to Recruit in return for a bribe.

The gap between the facts contended by Mr. Ezoe's defense team as a basis for demonstrating his innocence and the facts that the court accepted as reason to find Mr. Ezoe guilty was actually not that wide. The following is an overview of what transpired:

In September 1985, Recruit was considering the purchase of a supercomputer for its computer time-sharing business operations. The selection process was narrowed down to a Cray system and a Fujitsu FACOM VP-400. The company decided on the Fujitsu.

At this point, Cray was out of contention. Immediately, Cray took steps to restore its chances, this time working through its connections at NTT. Three days after Recruit ordered its Fujitsu system, Recruit made the decision, on its own, to purchase a second supercomputer—this time a Cray system. In other words, Recruit had decided to purchase not one but two supercomputers, systems that at the time came with a super-hefty price tag of around one billion yen each.

The original plan was that Recruit would buy this supercomputer directly from Cray, but in the course of events Recruit decided that the system would be procured through NTT. This change of procedure was not Recruit's idea, however; the notion was conceived by people at NTT and broached to Recruit.

At the time, there was serious friction plaguing U.S.–Japanese trade relations. NTT, despite having recently become privatized, had been pointed to by the U.S. government as a symbol of the closed nature of the Japanese market. The company was about to send its president, Hisashi Shinto, to the United States for discussions on the issue, and it was aware that if no progress was forthcoming, the company would be pilloried by the U.S. government, which had suggested the possibility of import sanctions against Japan. As a result, September 1985 was a time when NTT was under severe pressure to boost its procurements from the United States.

The idea of Recruit purchasing a Cray supercomputer through NTT, coming precisely at this juncture, was a stroke of genius for NTT. Not only were supercomputers an item that the U.S. government had been focusing upon in trade negotiations, if peripheral equipment were purchased at the same time, in one stroke NTT would be able to push its procurement record up dramatically by more than one billion yen. The upshot was that when Mr. Shinto soon after arrived in the United States, he was able to announce that NTT was purchasing a Cray supercomputer.

Meanwhile Mr. Ezoe, who had been approached by people at NTT about the scheme, had his own reasons for agreeing to their proposal. First, he was eager to cooperate with NTT; second, he sincerely hoped to contribute, even in a small way, to easing U.S.–Japanese trade frictions, which had become a prickly political issue. Neither Mr. Ezoe's abrupt decision to purchase a Cray supercomputer nor his positive response to the equally abrupt suggestion that Recruit buy it through NTT would have occurred without NTT's problem vis-à-vis international procurements.

The problem surrounding Recruit's purchase of the Cray supercomputer through NTT was in essence a problem that traced back to Mr. Ezoe's desire to save NTT from its plight. The court itself made no denial of this fact.

After Mr. Ezoe agreed to buy the Cray supercomputer through NTT, NTT, as would seem appropriate, performed a number of duties in conjunction with the system's adoption. The duties were limited to tasks necessary to get the Cray system up and running to serve the needs of Recruit's computer time-sharing business operations. NTT did not input any special expertise of a proprietary nature; all tasks performed were in fulfillment of its contract with Recruit.

The court acknowledged, without argument, that the duties NTT had performed in conjunction with the adoption of the supercomputer were not of a kind that could be labeled as "special favors" extended to Recruit.

These, in a nutshell, can be said to be the facts relating to the supercomputer matter. These facts notwithstanding, in its final ruling the court concluded that the duties performed by NTT were in part measures conducted to support and cooperate with Recruit. It also concluded that the sale of Recruit Cosmos shares to members of NTT management constituted bribery provided as a token of appreciation for NTT's performance of said duties.

The dividing line between conviction and acquittal in the instance of the NTT route and the supercomputer matter was thus the completely different assessments by the court and by the defense team—despite virtually identical fact-findings. (To be more precise, the divergent assessments also owed heavily to differing legal interpretations of the NTT Law, but owing to their complexity, this might not be the place to discuss it.)

Was the determination of guilt by the court correct? Was the defense wrong? What evidence could the court have relied on to justify its guilty verdict?

Let me go back a bit, to August 2002, when I was writing the closing argument in the Recruit case. After completing my draft concerning the supercomputer matter, I asked my wife to read over what I had written. At the time, my wife had been working in my law office doing clerical work for only a few months; she had had no prior experience in legal work. At the time of the media saturation of the Recruit case—between 1988 and 1989—she had been studying for her college entrance exams, so she had little time to follow media reports on the case, nearly all of which fueled suspicions of guilt. In short, my wife was a legal amateur who possessed almost no knowledge about the Recruit affair.

After she had read my draft, the first thing out of her mouth was, "Mr. Ezoe'll be found innocent, I assume?"

I was completely surprised by the directness of her response, so much so that without thinking I said, "No, he probably won't get off." At the time, all defendants charged as accomplices in the Recruit scandal had had their convictions finalized without exception based on admission of the facts claimed by the prosecutors. I am embarrassed to say that with the ramparts seemingly set firmly in place, it seemed impossible to hope that the court would hand down an innocent verdict even in part.

Needless to say, the document my wife had read was a summary of the facts as claimed by the defense. But under the circumstances, can one dismiss the honest impression of my wife—who had had no connection to court affairs, whose thinking had not been tinged by media coverage, and who ingenuously concluded, as a layperson with no preconceptions, that the events related to the supercomputer issue warranted a verdict of innocence—as the shallow thinking of an amateur? On the contrary, isn't it possible that the guileless sense of a layperson might be able to grasp essential truths better than that of people, including myself, who work in legal fields—judges, prosecutors, lawyers—who tend to be chained to presuppositions?

On the appointed date for presenting the final arguments in the Recruit case, each member of the defense team read his prepared remarks to the court. I was responsible for the supercomputer matter in conjunction with the "NTT route" as well as the "council member appointment" matter relating to the "Ministry of Education route."

In brief, the "council member appointment" matter centered around a number of people at Recruit, Mr. Ezoe among them, who had been appointed to serve on various councils, conference committees, etc. under the aegis of the Ministry of Education. A special investigation team from the Tokyo Public Prosecutors Office alleged that the appointments of Recruit personnel to these councils worked to the advantage of Recruit's business activities, and claimed that the appointments constituted favors. The truth of the matter, however, was that the ministry, which had been having difficulty finding appropriate candidates to serve on its councils, had itself chosen to appoint Recruit personnel so that the ministry might avail itself of the company's data relating to education—and Recruit had acquiesced to that request.

As with the supercomputer issue, this too was essentially a case of Recruit offering its support and cooperation—in this instance, to the Ministry of Education.

To return to that day when the final arguments were presented to the court: As I was reading from my prepared text, from time to time I would hear what sounded like titters of laughter coming from the visitors' gallery—which was largely filled with journalists. Meanwhile, from the prosecutors' table across from the defense team, the chief prosecutor—who had a fierce appearance even under normal circumstances—was directing a piercing, severe gaze toward me.

At the time, I was a young, callow attorney with but seven years' legal experience, and at each mention of various "facts" alleged by the special investigation squad, I stated that these "facts" were at extreme odds with what a layman's perceptions would be. I went back and re-read these final arguments as I was writing this chapter, and I was struck—and slightly embarrassed—by my scathing comments and the number of times I charged that the prosecution was "at odds with a layman's perceptions" and that its "claims deliberately attempt to distort everyday common sense." I stated this on no less than twenty occasions. No wonder the prosecutor was seething.

These, however, were the true feelings I had long felt personally toward the picture painted as "The Recruit Scandal" and grandiosely framed in the name of "social justice." At least insofar as the supercomputer issue and the council appointments are concerned, labeling the events as "special favors extended to Recruit" was like hanging the painting upside-down. Reality had been turned on its head.

The story does not end there.

Half a year after the final arguments were presented, on March 3, 2003, we were in court again to hear the verdict. The court's findings obliterated the faint ray of hope I had held, and Mr. Ezoe was declared guilty on all counts as most people expected.

If that were the full extent of it, the outcome in a sense would have fallen within the scope of cynical expectation. But there was something else. When the presiding judge pronounced the court's ruling in reference to the areas I had been in charge of—and *only* in reference to those areas—he made a point of stating that the contention of the defense attorney—that is, myself—that the prosecution's view ran counter to a layman's perceptions was "unacceptable." As the judge read the verdict, I got the distinct feeling that he was staring at me with contempt. Even as I wondered whether this was in my imagination, my fellow members of the defense team had the same feeling.

Why was the court was being so vindictive? Just because a member of the defense team had contended repeatedly that prosecution's allegations ran counter to a layperson's perceptions and that the court had swallowed these allegations whole, was that a reason for the court to inject repeated comments stressing that the prosecution's allegations *did not* run counter to a layman's perceptions? Had a nerve been hit?

After the trial, I never had occasion to speak with that presiding judge, so I do not know what his real intentions were. But looking back over the events today, now that the lay judge system has gotten under way, I sense that his message that day was that fact-finding by professional judges *does not* at all run counter to a layman's perception and is in fact conducted properly. And, concomitantly, the message may have been to proclaim his pride as a professional judge loudly.

After the verdict was handed down in Mr. Ezoe's case, the Justice System Reform Council, in its final report in June 2001, recommended elevating popular trust in the justice system through such measures as the introduction of systems whereby citizens could participate in judicial proceedings, centering on the introduction of the lay judge system. Mr. Ezoe's ruling thus came precisely at a time when specific work was under way to enact legislation to usher in the lay judge system. Exactly one year after Mr. Ezoe's verdict was passed down, the bill on legislation concerning participation by lay judges in criminal trials was submitted to the Diet.

Even now, I cannot help thinking that had the Recruit case been tried under a justice system in which ordinary citizens took part, Mr. Ezoe, at least where the supercomputer and council appointment matters are concerned, would have been acquitted.

Acquittals in Two Mock Trials

Seven and a half years have now passed since the verdict was handed down against Mr. Ezoe, and recently the period of his suspended sentence has drawn to a quiet close. In the interim I left Tokyo, where I was registered as an attorney, and relocated to an outlying city where the number of lawyers relative to population is much lower. I went about my work, and soon the day marking the start of the lay judge system arrived.

I might mention that in Shizuoka, the prefecture where I have my law office, owing to geography—the prefecture is spread out broadly west to east—and the nearly even distribution of the population, of considerable size, in the prefecture's western, central, and eastern sectors, lay judge trials are conducted at three courts within the same prefecture—the Shizuoka District Court Headquarters, the Hamamatsu Branch, and the Numazu Branch.

Starting two years ago, in preparation for the launch of the lay judge system, all three courts carried out repeated mock trials in collaboration with their respective local public prosecutors offices and bar associations. Mock trials were conducted at the Hamamatsu Branch to which I belong, with participating citizens—the lay judges—serving in their role through the cooperation of local businesses.

A system in which ordinary citizens participate in criminal trials as judicators marks a totally new experience not only for the citizens but also for those of us engaged in legal practice: lawyers, judges, and prosecutors alike. Among members of the legal profession, opinions on the wisdom of conducting lay judge trials are truly diverse, and even now opposition remains strong. In all honesty, I was skeptical in the beginning.

Varying opinions aside, mock trials were carried out all across Japan, and although the trials may have been simulations, actually participating in them seems to have brought many issues to light for the first time.

In Hamamatsu, four mock trials were held. In one, I played the role of a defendant on trial for homicide. In the end the lay judges found me innocent and I was cleared of the charges. In another mock trial, conducted with the procedures that would be used in real lay judge trials, the defendant was also acquitted. These outcomes have made me entertain positive expectations for the lay judge system. Whereas until now criminal trials by professional judges have inflexibly handed down rulings as "decrees from on high," I hope the new system will glow brilliantly with the common sense of a layperson.

To digress slightly, presently I am a member of the defense team in the "Hakamada case." On June 30, 1966, the managing director of a miso manufacturing plant in the town of Shimizu, now part of Shizuoka City, in Shizuoka Prefecture, was murdered, along with three family members, at his home, which was then set on fire. Iwao Hakamada, an employee at the miso plant who lived in the company dormitory, located on the second story of the plant, near to the manager's home, was charged as perpetrator of the crime.

Hakamada was arrested on August 18, 1966, after which for days on end he underwent interrogation so intense it could fall under the category of torture. In spite of peak summer heat, the door to the interrogation room was shut tightly, transforming the room into a steam bath. Even amid these conditions, Hakamada would not back off against a battery of police officers who had the freedom of leaving the room when the heat got unbearable. There were times when Hakamada was not allowed to leave the interrogation room to have a meal or go to the toilet. After undergoing this harsh interrogation for an average of twelve hours a day, he finally, twenty days after his arrest, signed his name to a statement confessing to the crime.

In his district court trial, Hakamada was claimed to have been wearing pajamas at the time of the crime. (This was also alleged in the "confession" signed under duress.) But roughly a year after he was charged in the case, in late August 1967, five blood-stained items of clothing were found in a miso tank—a tank that the police were assumed to have searched immediately after the crime took place. At that point, prosecutors changed their cause of action—which is to say, the "facts" of the case—so that these five items of clothing were what the perpetrator had been wearing at the time of the crime.

That the most important evidence in such a heinous crime was discovered at the crime scene more than a year later is difficult to fathom. In addition, several matters relating to the five items of clothing were highly irregular. For example, the items included a pair of briefs, *suteteko* (long underwear similar to longjohns), and trousers, and while all were blood-stained, blood traces were found over the widest area on the *suteteko*— which would have been *under* the trousers. Furthermore, traces of type-B blood were detected on the briefs but not on either the trousers or *suteteko*. If this were the clothing drenched with the blood of the victim, then why was the victim's particular blood type detected only on the briefs, which would have been worn closest to the assailant's body?

Given that the "confession" had been extracted under torture, coupled with irregularities of the most important evidence being discovered a year later, plus the condition of that evidence, it would be only logical to wonder whether Hakamada was the real culprit. The court, however, refused to lend an ear to Hakamada's pleas of innocence and, without responding to the many doubts clouding the case, handed down a death sentence—a sentence finalized in 1980 after the case passed through the Tokyo High Court and the Tokyo Supreme Court. Even now, the court remains adamantly reluctant to reopen the case and answer Hakamada's pleas for a retrial.

When the Tokyo Supreme Court decided against reopening the case in August 2004, in explaining its decision, it stated that the final ruling did not mean that it had been concluded that the perpetrator had consistently been wearing all five items of clothing in a "normal" manner; for example, the possibility existed that within the course of the crime the offender may have removed his trousers! This was the court's answer to the simple doubt as to why the blood type found on the briefs had not been detected on the *suteteko* or trousers.

Clearly, to say the possibility exists that the perpetrator of the crime—which took place at a home in a residential area, where the murderer stabbed four members of a family to death and then set fire to their home using a combination of gasoline and motor oil—removed his trousers partway through his crime can hardly be considered reasonable against the yardstick of common sense. I cannot help thinking that professional judges, who have had a monopoly on judgments under the criminal justice system, feared that a defendant's innocence would be exposed.

But, as I described earlier, in the mock trials conducted in Hamamatsu prior to implementation of the lay judge system, deliberations in which lay judges participated resulted in an innocent verdict for two of the four defendants. The objective of the lay judge system—to produce results reflecting a layperson's perceptions—was not a pipe dream after all.

In the first mock case where the defendant was acquitted, the point of dispute was the credibility of the testimony given by a witness to the crime. The prosecutor and defense attorney engaged in a battle of opinions concerning the credibility of the individual, and the panel of judges—six lay judges and three professional judges—concluded that the witness's testimony lacked credibility.

According to the defense attorney in this mock trial, among the reasons the defendant was acquitted was because the witness's testimony had been so "clear and specific." This is one consideration that would be unlikely to come up in the setting of a criminal trial adjudicated by professional judges, where "clear and specific" testimony would be a powerful weapon to support the credibility of the witness. Typically, the prosecution would focus on demonstrating just how "clear and specific" the testimony was, and the defense would rack its brains to show how, although the testimony might on the surface seem clear and specific, it was vague and lacked solid basis. In the mock trial, though, the circumstance of such "clear and specific" testimony was taken as reason to conclude that it actually lacked credibility. This, the defense attorney said, was striking.

Here is what made the difference: the witness, according to the mock scenario, had been drinking at the time he witnessed the crime. The ordinary citizens who were lay judges harbored genuine doubts as to whether a witness who had been drinking was really capable of explaining what happened as clearly and specifically as he had. To embrace doubts of this nature would seem altogether natural and reasonable, and it is precisely this natural and reasonable aspect—this sound perception of the layman— that I believe tends to lack in traditional criminal trials.

Even in traditional proceedings, there is no paucity of contentions by a defense attorney that a witness's testimony is excessively specific to the point of being unnatural. Nonetheless, with the exception of occasions when that testimony is so clearly unnatural in that it does not accord with the objective circumstances of the crime scene (for example, if a witness testified that he saw something that was physically impossible for him to see), it was fatuous to hope that such contentions would be accepted without fuss by the court.

In the mock trial, however, the participating laymen, who throughout their lives had had no connection whatsoever to criminal trials, indicated, with logic and candor, their doubts about something that did not match their perception of "natural" based on their own everyday experience. The lay judge system thus offers the possibility of injecting what the world at large considers to be "natural" into the context of criminal trials.

The second mock trial where the defendant was found innocent is the one in which I played the role of a defendant charged with homicide. The scenario had me playing a schizophrenic, and delusions caused by my mental illness allegedly figured heavily in my criminal motive. As one would expect, the point in dispute was whether I could be held criminally responsible for my actions.

In real lay judge trials, the deliberations involving lay judges are kept completely secret, and lay judges are forbidden to reveal what actually took place forever after. In the mock trials, however, exchanges between the court judges and the lay judges outside the courtroom, including when court proceedings were temporarily halted for breaks, were openly made known. In my mock trial too, it was possible to monitor how the impressions gained by the lay judges changed minute by minute depending on how the court proceedings were going.

In this mock trial, a statement had been drawn up during the investigation phase when the defendant admitted to the crime. Since the scenario had it that the defense attorney would not voice objections regarding the interrogation that had led to the statement, the prosecution submitted the confession relatively early in the court proceedings. Statements prepared by the investigating side of course are not word-for-word accounts of the defendant's explanation; they are statements presenting the general drift of what the investigator was told, and typically they are very cogently written. As a result, when the mock lay judges were asked their impressions immediately after the statement of confession was read, they leaned strongly on the side of sensing no problem with the defendant's mental capacity.

That impression changed dramatically after they observed the subsequent questioning of the defendant. Because the point in dispute was the capacity of a mentally unstable defendant to bear responsibility for his actions, what he said or the attitude he displayed in the courtroom could potentially affect the outcome significantly. It had therefore been agreed beforehand that except for where the lay judges were concerned, the questions of the prosecution and answers from the defendant would faithfully reproduce, without modification, the questions and answers from the actual court proceedings which this mock trial had been modeled on. As the defendant, I was to act out my part exactly as it was written in the "script," my responses to questions making no sense, their content totally disoriented and flying off into a world of delusion. If I do say so myself, I acted the part of a schizophrenic defendant flawlessly, practically word-for-word as written in the script. The lay judges, finding my scripted remarks to be incoherent beyond comprehension, asked a string of questions in an attempt to make sense of my testimony. Their questions were unscripted and thus unexpected.

During the deliberations conducted during the break immediately after my testimony, the lay judges began voicing their shared impression that the defendant clearly deviated from what one would consider normal. One commented that he found it inconceivable that the defendant would have been capable of stating what was written in his "confession," despite the defense attorney's having indicated no argument with it.

Here were lay judges telling one another of their doubts concerning the prosecution based on the exchanges that had taken place within the courtroom. This was entirely new to me.

One striking thing demonstrated in the innocent verdict handed down in the two mock trials is that the free and simple way lay judges assess situations did not exist in the traditional realm of criminal trials monopolized by members of the legal professions. Lay judges have the potential to cast "reasonable doubt" from a completely different perspective.

Another thing I felt was that the lay judge system functions in a way that enables professional judges to see, right in front of them, how laymen who participate as lay judges embrace honest, "normal" doubts. Though it may be going too far to say, I would even suggest that with traditional criminal proceedings court judges, who in the execution of their professional duties rarely have a chance to leave the courthouse, have no alternative but to consider whether the judgments they render coincide with "the layman's perception." In the deliberations undertaken during the two mock trials, the professional judges should have witnessed firsthand that even opinions difficult to accept in earlier criminal proceedings are in fact supported by a majority of ordinary citizens. As such, it should become easier for professional judges to leap the difficult hurdle of handing down a not-guilty verdict.

Eliminating "Prejudgments"

Now that the lay judge system has been launched, my great hope is that it will drive reform of Japan's rigid criminal justice proceedings.

One must keep in mind, however, that this system injecting a layman's perspective into judicial decisions also harbors a major risk. This is the risk that the deluge of media that is characteristic of real life today will give rise to prejudgments of defendants in criminal trials and impede discovery of the truth through criminal process.

Not long ago, unexpected developments brought the case of Kazuyoshi Miura, the businessman who had been arrested, convicted, and then acquitted in conjunction with the slaying of his wife in Los Angeles in 1981, back into the limelight. The Tokyo High Court, on finding Miura innocent on July 1, 1998 (a verdict subsequently finalized by the Supreme Court), included the following comments in its ruling:

> This case, referred to as the "Los Angeles Shooting Scandal," became the center of a wild media frenzy, with the weeklies, entertainment tabloids and TV talk shows taking the lead in reporting on the case with relentless zeal. In cases of this sort, in general there is an unavoidable trend for those on the reporting side to cast suspicion on the accused without adequately considering whether or not the evidence on which their reporting is based has sufficient certainty to stand up to critical cross-examination and retain high credibility.
>
> In the present case, however, in subsequently examining the evidence in court it came to light that the evidence was extremely open to question and not as simple as had been widely reported. . . .
>
> However, even when the examination of evidence concludes that the evidence is open to question, the initial impression held by those who are on the receiving end of such reporting is not easily obliterated.
>
> On the contrary, some people may judge the case based on their first impression and suspect that the court's findings must be wrong.
>
> In order to avert misunderstandings and mistrust of this kind, I

keenly sense the importance of first pointing out the distinction between facts made clear through solid evidence that has stood up to critical examination in court and reported "facts" that ultimately are unsubstantiated and mere speculation, so as to enable a reconsideration of the facts in the case based on the evidence.

This ruling handed down by the Tokyo High Court came more than a year before the Justice System Reform Council was established and deliberations on bringing citizens into the justice system got under way in earnest. The passage almost foresees the coming of the lay judge system.

More than a few incidents of false accusation resulting from media reporting have come to light, the Matsumoto sarin gas incident (in which members of Aum Shinrikyo cult released sarin gas in Matsumoto, Nagano Prefecture, in 1994, resulting in eight deaths) among them. Nonetheless, even today crime reporting continues to be largely based on information provided by investigating agencies, and there is no end to cases in which an innocent person is portrayed as though he were a suspect and presumed guilty.

Were the lay judge system to continue without changes, solid verification would also have to be undertaken regarding the problem of an "impression of guilt" being formed in advance as a result of media reports mixing fact and fiction, confounding the hope for the sound perceptions of the layman to be reflected in criminal justice proceedings. Especially, it must be recognized that, as the Tokyo High Court correctly indicated, once the media paints someone as a criminal, that prejudgment is not easily erased.

In operating the lay judge trial system, it will at all times be necessary to ask what reality lurks behind the pleasant-sounding phrase "citizens' participation in meting out justice." This reality is that citizens, not professional judges, now shoulder the responsibility of sentencing to prison or, at times, condemning to death someone whom the investigating agencies and media have labeled as a criminal but who might actually be innocent.

Problems with the Preparation of Statements

Back to the supercomputer matter:

In the Recruit case, a case in which many individuals were arrested and indicted, in a number of instances the scenario depicted by the special investigation unit of the Tokyo Public Prosecutors Office was ultimately rejected during the fact-finding processes and in the judgments handed down in multiple courts. The matter surrounding the supercomputer purchase in the NTT route was one example.

According to the special investigators' scenario, in choosing a supercomputer to purchase, Recruit considered both a Fujitsu FACOM VP-400 and a system made by Cray Research; Recruit opted to forgo the Cray system on the grounds it was technologically too advanced for Recruit to handle, and so decided on the Fujitsu system. The investigators claimed that Recruit subsequently secured a promise from NTT of technical support that would enable adoption of the Cray system, and with that support Recruit could put to use the Cray system it had earlier given up on. The premise that the Cray system was technologically too advanced for Recruit thus served as the impetus behind NTT's providing Recruit with special technical support, which is to say, "special favors."

In the subsequent trial proceedings, however, it was revealed, based on various materials and testimony, that no one who would have been involved in using the supercomputer at Recruit had ever offered the opinion that the Cray system was technologically too advanced. Ultimately, the Public Prosecutors Office itself, in presenting its final arguments, retracted its claims that the Cray system had been considered too sophisticated.

Why then did something of this kind take place? The whole problem stemmed from the fact that the special investigators from the Tokyo Public Prosecutors Office put together an erroneous scenario based on the investigation materials at their disposal. Having said that, I will concede that the investigators' error could be traced to a statement made by Mr. Ezoe himself on November 21, 1988, at a meeting of a special Lower House committee created to investigate the Recruit matter. As Mr. Ezoe himself revealed in writing, the reason he testified in the Diet that he had relied on NTT's technical support because Cray's technology was so advanced, was to conceal the fact that purchasing the Cray supercomputer through NTT was a quick resale scheme so that NTT could claim having engaged in international procurement.

It was perhaps inevitable that the special investigators should incorporate the hypothesis that the Cray system was technologically too advanced into their scenario as an important element for issuing indictments in connection with the NTT route. A deeper, more fundamental problem was waiting on the horizon, however. As described, the circumstance that no one at Recruit had ever indicated that the Cray supercomputer was technologically too advanced for Recruit was an objective fact that even the Public Prosecutors Office had to admit. Therefore, even if Mr. Ezoe had testified to that effect before the Diet, the Public Prosecutors Office's reputedly elite lineup of special investigators should have brought to light—through questioning of those involved—that what Mr. Ezoe had testified in the Diet had been incorrect.

Nevertheless, the statements prepared by the special investigators contained the identical statement—that Cray's system was technologically too advanced for Recruit to deal with. It had become practically a mantra. And it was those erroneous statements that were to be submitted to the court as evidence to prove the facts of the crime.

The problem is this: Once the special investigating agency has put together a scenario of events, no matter how much the concerned parties might contend the scenario is wrong, it never gets corrected. What is scarier is the frequency that this occurs and the large volume of statements that are prepared containing such erroneous scenarios.

Consider the "Nabari incident," a case dating back to 1961 in which five people at a community center meeting in Nabari, Mie Prefecture, died after drinking wine laced with a pesticide. The individual who was arrested and charged with the crime confessed under pressure during the investigation phase, but later retracted his confession and pleaded innocent throughout his trial. The district court initially found him innocent, only to have the ruling overturned by the Nagoya High Court and a death sentence handed down. Recent hearings have been held at the same court to hear the convicted party's request for a retrial, and judgments have been split, with one deciding to launch a new trial and another flatly rejecting the retrial request. Presently the case is under special appeal to the Supreme Court.

In this case, the timing of when the poisoned wine was brought into the community center had been a major focus. When questioned immediately after the incident, the townspeople offered a variety of explanations; but as the investigation proceeded, gradually their testimony shifted to all match one other.

Two things are demonstrated by this: first, that investigators labor to find a scenario based on "evidence"; and second, that there actually exists a process whereby the investigators prepare "evidence"—that is to say, statements—to match the scenario they have come up with. Furthermore, as past examples have shown, this task of "coordinating statements" appears to be achieved quite easily, without physically detaining the people involved or resorting to unlawful means such as violence or threat.

Recently there have been a string of media reports of courts around the country rejecting the purported voluntariness of defendants' statements of confession drawn up during their investigation phase, and removing such statements from evidence. Also, public prosecutors offices, hoping to blunt the criticism of their interrogations conducted "behind closed doors," have begun recording their interrogations, albeit partially, either on audio tape or video.

Moves in these directions are in part linked to the implementation of the lay judge system. Debate surrounding the credibility of statements of confession are on the whole difficult to understand, and deliberations take too much time. Consequently, because of the problems that would be involved if lay judges had to deal with such prickly issues, there is a trend toward securing, in advance, ways that enable interrogations conducted behind closed doors to be checked by third parties. The issues surrounding how investigative agencies go about their interrogations are now being actively debated, and tangible results are gradually being achieved in the name of making such interrogations visible.

From our perspective as defense attorneys, however, such efforts to bring visibility to interrogations remain inadequate. As an example, preparation of flawed statements of confession of the kind associated with the supercomputer matter is not limited to individuals in custody. Statements taken from individuals who are not in custody and who are being questioned voluntarily as witnesses also include an equal measure of erroneous content conforming to the scenario of the special investigators.

With implementation of the lay judge system, laymen who live ordinary lives will now have significantly more contact with the statements drawn up by investigating agencies and what they claim in them. Under current circumstances, laymen who participate as lay judges could conceivably, and understandably, render mistaken verdicts against a defendant based on specious statements prepared by investigators.

If everyday citizens are to be made to shoulder the weighty responsibility of participating in criminal trials, it is necessary first to change how interrogations are conducted behind closed doors. At the very least, a system must be set in place that will enable lay judges, when they harbor the slightest doubt regarding the credibility of statements taken during the investigative phase, to examine objectively the circumstances under which the interrogations were conducted. Achieving full visibility of interrogations by investigating agencies—recording either on audio tape or video the entire interrogation process for all interrogations, whether or not of a criminal suspect, and not limiting the scope to preparation of statements only—is of the utmost urgency.

For the Defendant's Sake

By injecting the sound perspective of the layman, the lay judge system has the potential to change significantly the way criminal justice is meted out. That potential casts a ray of hope into an area of criminal justice that has tended to be rigid, breaking down barriers that have made it difficult for a defendant to have his plea of innocence accepted.

At the same time, having ordinary citizens participate in criminal trials runs the risk of losing the equanimity that the justice system has traditionally maintained in criminal trials: for example, by allowing the misguided predictions made by the media to be carried over into the trial proceedings, or for the trial outcome to be swayed by feelings emoted by victims or bereaved family members.

In this way, the lay judge system is not a cure-all. In order for the system to function more properly, it is necessary—not only for us in the legal professions, but also for ordinary citizens called to participate as lay judges as well as members of the media—to examine the results of trials thoroughly. Whether this nascent system will grow up to be hale and hearty and set down roots in Japanese society will depend on how serious our initiatives are.

In mulling how the system should function, we must not forget that a criminal trial is inherently a process that exists to protect the interests of the defendant. Going through a criminal trial is required whenever the nation exercises its right of punishment against a criminal offender. Proper functioning is essential in order to prevent the state's right of punishment— a serious adverse disposition—from being carried out mistakenly without regard for the presupposed facts, or arbitrarily by powerful elements.

In the system currently in place, defendants do not have the right to choose between a trial by lay judges and one by professional judges. As such, defendants who are charged with certain types of serious crime are compelled to entrust their vital right to a fair trial to six "amateurs" who have had no special education or training in criminal process and whose only credential is having been selected by a draw of lots. In a sense this is almost tantamount to gambling—with their lives. Under these circumstances, all parties involved—the lay judges and professional judges, prosecutors, and attorneys—must maintain strict awareness that their position is also entrusted with the defendant's rights. In order to conduct a truly fair trial under the lay judge system, the defendant's right to defend himself must not in any way be restricted.

In lay judge trials it is assumed that in the majority of cases a verdict will be reached after three consecutive days of court proceedings. This general rule is said to have been arrived at because any proceeding lasting more than three consecutive days would create undue burden on the lay judges. The courts are trying hard to stick to this timetable.

Keep in mind that, before a verdict can be reached, time is needed for the prosecution and the defense to express their views and for the judges and lay judges to deliberate. By this measure, the time actually allocated to court proceedings is thus limited to about two days. Also, for cases to be tried by lay judges, pre-trial procedures—where the judges, prosecution, and defense together narrow down the points of dispute and work out a schedule—are carried out prior to the start of the proceedings. Given these conditions, it has become necessary for the courts to request that the prosecution and the defense limit their time examining witnesses.

If criminal trials exist to protect the rights of the defendant, there is something perverse in the notion of giving precedence to the convenience of lay judges and limiting the duration of court proceedings. Where are our priorities? Indeed, there have been some instances where lay judges have expressed the view that the court proceedings were too brief and that they were unable to mull over the content of the verdict at sufficient length.

With respect to how court proceedings are carried out, there seems to be too much emphasis placed on making the proceedings "easy to understand" for the lay judges. Obviously lay judges need to understand the content of the proceedings well in order for them to apply their layman's wisdom, and prosecutors and defense lawyers should pursue such ease of understanding as an underlying premise.

That said, it is impossible to condone the notion of reducing the volume of information in a case to make proceedings more easily understood by lay judges. Reducing the volume of information can lead to paring away details and undermine the case's basic aspects. In that event, it would become more rather than less difficult for lay judges, who lack specialized knowledge in legal proceedings, to picture what took place in the case, raising the fear that this could obstruct the diverse values of the lay judges—each different in character and social experience—from being reflected in the criminal trial process. Were that to happen, the fundamental objectives for introducing the lay judge system would have been undercut and lay judges could come to serve as nothing more than adornment.

Furthermore, if a verdict is appealed in a case which lay judges have participated in the decision of, the view has been expressed that the appeals court, which is comprised solely of professional judges, should respect the verdict for reflecting the sense of ordinary citizens. An operational policy of this kind, however, could potentially infringe upon a defendant's rights. Verdicts involving lay judges are not in themselves sacred; they could conceivably have been reached in error. Why should that error go uncorrected?

From the perspective of guaranteeing a defendant's right of defense, the current lay judge system still seems fraught with problems. Once the lay judge system was introduced, it was a given that the system would place a burden on ordinary citizens. Lay judges must accept the burden as necessary to fulfilling their weighty responsibility in order to guarantee every defendant's right to receive a fair trial. It behooves all citizens who are eligible to serve as lay judges to affirm this right.

Etsuyoshi Izuta. Born in 1970. Passed the bar exam, 1993. Graduated from the University of Tokyo, Faculty of Law, entered the Legal Training and Research Institute of Japan,1994. Became Attorney at Law, registered with the Dai-ni Tokyo Bar Association, 1996. Shifted registry to the Shizuoka Bar Association, established Izuta Law Office, 2002. Established Libra Law Offices, 2005.

Currently affiliated with the Hamamatsu Branch of the Shizuoka Bar Association; member of the Hakamada Case Subcommittee of the Human Rights Protection Committee of the Japan Federation of Bar Associations.

VII

SIGNIFICANCE OF THE JAPAN LEGAL SUPPORT CENTER

The Court-Appointed Defense Counsel System in Crisis

Shozaburo Ishida, Attorney at Law

The Hidden Aspects of Justice System Reform

Six decades after Japan entered the postwar era, major changes are now being made to its justice system. With progress in the training of legal professionals at law schools, today the number of Japanese entering legal professions, particularly as defense lawyers, is increasing substantially.

New methods have also been introduced into court proceedings, as exemplified by the launch of the lay judge system in conjunction with criminal cases and of the industrial tribunal system in conjunction with labor-related cases. Initiatives are making rapid progress in the name of realizing a truly democratic justice system and improving the nation's legal services; for example, laws are being enacted to promote speedy trials, and measures are being taken to achieve more focused court proceedings in criminal trials through the adoption of new pre-trial procedures.

Questions remain, however, as to whether such reforms can be called reforms that truly serve in the public's interest, or whether lurking behind such measures is an attempt by the government to control the justice system, contrary to the principle of the separation of powers. In particular, the establishment of the Japan Legal Support Center (JLSC, also known as Houterasu) and the operation of the system of court-appointed defense lawyers under its direction will conceivably have a major impact on how criminal defense will be undertaken and how attorneys will operate their business.

I cannot help feeling that irreversible events affecting the Japanese public are going forward today in the largely unfamiliar realm of judicial administration.

Problems Arising from the Comprehensive Legal Support Act

In June 2004 the Comprehensive Legal Support Act was enacted as part of the Koizumi administration's reforms of the justice system. Under this Act, the Japan Legal Support Center was established in April 2006; JLSC operations got under way that October.

The Comprehensive Legal Support Act gave legislative form to a system that earlier had been referred to as the Legal Service Center. The objectives of the Act are described in Article 1:

> *Owing to the changes in the social and economic situation at home and abroad, the settlement of disputes based on laws has become increasingly more important. Bearing such in mind, the purpose of this Act shall be to contribute to the formation of a freer and fairer society by providing not only the basic principles, the responsibilities of the national and local government and other basic matters, but also the organization and operation of the Japan Legal Support Center which is the core body of comprehensive support, with respect to the implementation and the establishment of systems of comprehensive legal support to further facilitate the use of judicial decisions and other systems for the settlement of disputes based on laws, and to make it easier to receive support from attorneys at law and legal professional corporations, as well as judicial scriveners and other related legal experts and specialists.*

The Act's underlying basic principles are elaborated in Article 2:

> *The implementation of comprehensive legal support and the establishment of systems shall aim at creating a society in which the*

provision of information and support necessary to settle disputes based on laws concerning criminal as well as civil cases can be received nationwide.

For many years the Japan Federation of Bar Associations (JFBA) had been advocating expansion of the legal aid system and the creation of a system of court-appointed defense counsel for criminal suspects, so the enactment of the Comprehensive Legal Support Act, along with incorporation into the Code of Criminal Procedure (Article 37-2) of a new system of court-appointed lawyers for criminal suspects, was generally welcomed. It is thought to have already produced results to some extent.

When adoption of the Act was passed in the Diet on May 26, 2004, JFBA president Go Kajitani released a statement saying that the Act had been created for two purposes: to make it easier for the nation's citizens to avail of a system for resolving disputes by law, and to enable them to receive more readily the services of attorneys. Kajitani stated that the Act clarified the responsibilities of the nation and provided the basis for establishing the Japan Legal Support Center as a new organization to handle matters relating to legal aid in civil cases and court-appointed defense counsel comprehensively, and to take steps to counter the lack of adequate legal services in outlying regions, and to establish operations to support victims of crime. He pointed out that the JFBA had long been proactive in undertaking activities aimed at realizing what he called a "society in which anyone, anywhere, at any time could receive good-quality legal services," and in indicating where the nation's duties lay.

With the Act's adoption, Kajitani said this goal had finally been realized and was an achievement of significance and worthy of acclaim. A report issued by the JFBA's headquarters for promoting the Japan Legal Support Center similarly stated that the movement, centered on the JFBA, to realize court-appointed counsel for suspects accused of criminal acts had been carried on for many years, and its objectives and basic principles were congruous with those of justice system reforms targeting expanded legal access in civil and other areas. The report applauded the movement's successful implementation of justice system reforms, notably the establishment of the Comprehensive Legal Support Act.

Inarguably there are inadequacies in the newly launched system under which court-appointed defense counsel is assigned, under certain conditions, to people in detention who have been accused of a crime but not yet indicted, as a complement to the system for assigning counsel to defendants after indictment: for one thing, the system applies only to certain types of crime. Nonetheless, creation of the system itself marks a step forward for the criminal justice system.

When the system's creation is examined in tandem with how the JLSC works, however, can we applaud the result without reservations?

With regard to the selection of court-appointed counsel in criminal cases, especially, the Act stipulates:

> *When a court-appointed defense counsel et al. is to be appointed based on the provisions of the Code of Criminal Procedure or the Juvenile Law, the court, presiding judge or judge shall request the JLSC to nominate and notify candidates for court-appointed defense counsel et al.* (Article 38-1)

If the court permits only court-appointed counsel nominated by the JLSC, is not such a system of concern in terms of how, basically, the nation's justice system will now operate?

Problems in the JLSC's Organization

The Comprehensive Legal Support Act stipulates the creation of an independent administrative agency—the Japan Legal Support Center—as an organization to serve as the nucleus of the nation's comprehensive legal support program. The JLSC is charged with functions including legal aid, legal consultation, nomination of court-appointed defense counsel, and training in legal affairs.

The organizational makeup and other features of the JLSC, as defined in the Comprehensive Legal Support Act, are as follows:

The capital of the JLSC shall be furnished by the national government at the time of its establishment. (Article 17-1)

The Minister of Justice shall appoint the JLSC's president and inspectors. (Article 24-1 and 24-2)

The JLSC's president shall select and appoint the organization's executive director(s). (Article 24-4)

Insofar as application of the Penal Code and other penal provisions is concerned, the officers and staff of the JLSC shall be deemed to be staff engaged in public services based on laws and regulations. (Article 28)

The Act also sets down detailed provisions regarding the JLSC's "affairs" and nominations of court-appointed defense counsel. First, the JLSC's affairs are said to require approval from the Minister of Justice.

An Evaluation Commission of the JLSC shall be established within the Ministry of Justice to deal with affairs related to the JLSC. The Commission shall take charge of . . . matters concerning evaluation related to the business performance of the JLSC. (Article 19)

When commencing business, the JLSC shall prepare a statement of operation procedures and obtain the approval of the Minister of Justice. [The statement of operation procedures is to include] matters concerning contracts with attorneys at law, matters concerning the nomination of candidates for court-appointed defense counsel et al. and court-appointed attorneys at law for victims and notice to the courts. (Article 34)

The JLSC shall establish the rules for the handling of legal affairs to be handled by contract attorneys at law et al. (. . . rules for the handling of legal affairs) and shall obtain the approval of the Minister of Justice. The rules for the handling of legal affairs shall contain matters concerning the criteria for the handling of legal affairs by contract attorneys at law et al., matters concerning measures to be taken if contract attorneys at law et al. violate their duties stipulated by the contract and other matters provided for by an Ordinance of the Ministry of Justice. (Article 35)

According to Article 38-2 and 38-3:

When a court-appointed defense counsel et al. is to be appointed based on the provisions of the Code of Criminal Procedure or the Juvenile Law, the court, presiding judge or judge shall request the JLSC to nominate and notify candidates for court-appointed defense counsel et al. . . . . When requested as under the provision set forth in the preceding paragraph, the JLSC shall nominate candidates for court-appointed defense counsel et al. out of the court-appointed contract defense counsel and notify the court, presiding judge or judge thereof. When a court-appointed contract defense counsel is appointed as court-appointed defense counsel et al. the JLSC shall have the court-appointed contract defense counsel handle the affairs of the court-appointed defense counsel et al. pursuant to the provisions of the contract concerned.

In the following instance, too, approval from the Minister of Justice is required:

The JLSC shall stipulate the contract concerning the affairs handled by court-appointed defense counsel et al. . . . and shall obtain the Minister of Justice's approval for the contract. (Article 36)

I have quoted the Act at length, my intention being to present an objective overview of the system.

While content relating to regulations governing legal affairs, contract provisions, and other matters is still being worked out (a progress report is presented in the February 1, 2006, issue of *Jurist* magazine, available in Japanese only), an objective look at the foregoing passages from the Act should suffice to demonstrate that the system is problematic.

Government Interference in Attorneys' Affairs

The problem is self-evident: "comprehensive legal support," as it is called, comes entirely under the supervision of the Ministry of Justice, which is to say, the government.

This should perhaps be accepted as a matter of course given that providing comprehensive legal support is defined as a duty of the state and the state has budgeted vast sums for the benefit of its citizens. (In its 2009 budget, the government set aside 26.2 billion yen in expenses relating to the JLSC, including 10.4 billion yen earmarked for outsourcing work to secure court-appointed legal counsel.)

Inherently, however, business relating to the administration of justice, especially work performed by attorneys at law, should be carried out independently of the government. This is logical from the standpoint of the separation of powers and, most importantly, from the perspective that it is only when defense activities are conducted free from state supervision that the interests of the client can be protected. This is clear from the law known as the Attorney Act.

In order to become an attorney at law, a lawyer's registration on the roll of attorneys held by the JFBA is required. The JFBA, seeking to maintain the dignity of attorneys and legal professional corporations and to improve and advance the business of attorneys in reflection of their mission and professional duties, performs duties pursuant to guidance and supervision of, and communication with, attorneys and bar associations. In the event that an attorney commits an act undermining such dignity—violating the law or bar association rules, damaging the order or trust of the bar association to which he belongs, or any other indiscretion within or outside the scope of his professional duties—he receives disciplinary punishment from the bar association of which he is a member.

Needless to say, the JFBA and various bar associations around the country are organizations independent of the state, and attorneys submit to the guidance, supervision, and punishment of the JFBA or their bar association. They perform their professional duties independent of state institutions—in the interest of the nation's citizens.

The Comprehensive Legal Support Act, however, attempts to infuse aspects alien both to the essential nature of how attorneys carry out their professional duties and to the basic principles of the Attorney Act.

Cases Involving Court-Appointed Defense Counsel, and Autonomy of Defense

The problems inherent in the Comprehensive Legal Support Act are especially apparent in criminal defense situations conducted, at the most fundamental level, from a position contrary to that of the government.

In Japan, more than sixty percent of all criminal cases are defended by court-appointed attorneys. Under the current system, the court-appointed defense counsel operates under funds budgeted to the Supreme Court. Attorney recommendations are made by the bar associations. The Ministry of Justice has no involvement in those recommendations, and the government neither monitors nor supervises related procedures.

The comprehensive legal support system, however, attempts to place operation of the system of court-appointed defense counsel under the supervision, approval, and aegis of the Minister of Justice. A major problem in the way the JLSC nominates court-appointed defense counsel is the stipulation that candidates are to be nominated from among "contract attorneys at law." This is the term applied to attorneys who enter a contract with the JLSC pursuant to the handling of affairs as a court-appointed lawyer (Article 30-1-3). If the court is allowed to select as appointed defense counsel only from among attorneys nominated by the JLSC, this means that all court-appointed attorneys will be regulated by their contracts with the JLSC. This completely erodes all autonomy in the performance of legal defense.

A variety of counterarguments have been put forward. For example, insofar as application of laws is concerned, supporters of the Comprehensive Legal Support Act say that it systematically guarantees the autonomy and independence of criminal defense by virtue of its stipulations that *consideration shall always be given to the special characteristics of the duties of attorneys at law and related legal experts and specialists* (Article 12) and that *a contract attorney at law et al. shall independently fulfill his or her duties* (Article 33-1). Or they point out that the heads of the local branches of the JLSC are to be appointed from attorneys who have been recommended by the local bar association, and the autonomy of attorneys and the bar associations is inherently guaranteed by their authority over personnel issues.

Nevertheless, even if supervision under the legal support program may not equate to intervention in specific individual duties, so long as the attorneys who are to carry out such duties are brought into the system under contract, there can be no true independence. On the contrary, the Comprehensive Legal Support Act admits that such stipulations are by their own nature threatening to such independence. Furthermore, concerning both the guarantee of autonomy by virtue of the authority over personnel issues and the JFBA's involvement in the system's operation, these are not matters determined as part of the system, but only simple, groundless hopes.

The upshot is that both the prosecution and the defense, the two opposing sides in a criminal trial, are to be placed under the control of the government. It should be all too clear that so long as this fundamental structure exists, real defense by suspects and defendants in conflict with the government's position cannot be possible.

It is self-evident that the defense in a criminal case must be built upon a relationship of trust between the counsel and the client. It is only when trust exists that the client feels he can tell everything to his attorney, thereby laying the groundwork of a true defense.

Under the comprehensive legal support system, because court-appointed defense counsel is assigned by the state, the strong possibility exists that these appointees will be viewed with distrust by suspects and defendants. Furthermore, the possibility arises that the defense counsel could actually become an adversary of his client. It is a mistake in the first place to entrust the administration of these duties to an independent administrative agency—an agency that by definition exists for the purpose of conducting affairs *"efficiently and effectively"* (Act on General Rules for Independent Administrative Agency, Article 2).

What is behind the Comprehensive Legal Support Act is nothing but an effort to place attorneys, whose activities should inherently be free and independent, under state management. This certainly will not work in the interests of the nation's citizens.

Postscript

A central focus of the lay judge trial system launched on May 21, 2009, is the achievement of swift court proceedings. Proceedings in the courtroom, excluding pre-trial procedures, now average between three and five days—significantly shorter than previous trials. The new system thus appears to be producing real results.

Having personally been through a trial that dragged on for more than thirteen years, I believe the new system of swift court proceedings is basically positive. And yet, while achieving swift proceedings is clearly an issue needing to be addressed, what is most important in a trial is handing down a fair ruling. In reforming the Japanese justice system, what I believe should be sought is simultaneous achievement of both swift court proceedings *and* a fair trial. A justice system cannot be ideal if one of those two elements is missing.

Based on this perspective, in this volume I have written a frank account, based on my own experience, of those areas of the current justice system—including pre-trial interrogations—that I would like to see changed. I have also pointed out, at random, what changes I believe might be made to make the system better.

Admittedly, I never studied law and my knowledge of legal matters is sketchy, so legal professionals may find some of what I say to be odd. My hope is that I might be granted some leniency in that regard and have my opinions be seen as coming from someone who has actually sat in the defendant's seat.

The shelves of Japanese bookstores already have an ample array of books expressing opposition to the new lay judge system. In my own view, though, the new system is, at the least, substantially better than the one it replaces.

I also admire how well the jury system functions in the United States.

Opinions toward the lay judge system are strongly divided. Even among attorneys, who are specialists in law, opinions span a wide spectrum—as should be clear to the reader of this book.

Japan's Code of Criminal Procedure was put into effect in January 1949—over sixty years ago. It is because the Code is viewed to be problematic that the current bold changes are being implemented. Bold changes inevitably create some confusion. I am confident that as the new changes are modified over the next several years, the outcome will be a new system that will be strongly supported by the Japanese public.

In closing, I would like to thank Takuji Yokote of Chuokoron-Shinsha, Inc. for his support in the publication of the original Japanese-language edition. I would like to express my gratitude to Masayuki Uchiyama, senior editorial director at Kodansha International, who kindly offered me a chance to publish this book after the publication of *Where Is the Justice*, my first book in English. Finally, I would like to express my sincere appreciation to translator Robert A. Muntzer and editors Junko Kawakami and Elmer Luke of this English version for their enormous contribution.

HIROMASA EZOE
November 2010

ABOUT THE AUTHORS

Hiromasa Ezoe

Born in 1936. Graduated in educational psychology from the University of Tokyo. Established Daigaku Kokoku Co. Ltd., the predecessor of today's Recruit Co., Ltd., 1960. Launched the Ezoe Scholarship Society Foundation, 1971. Resigned as chairman of Recruit, 1988. Has served as chairman of the Ezoe Scholarship Society Foundation and director for La Voce Incorporated, which promotes opera and classical music performances. Published *Where Is the Justice?: Media Attacks, Prosecutorial Abuse, and My 13 Years in Japanese Court* in English from Kodansha International, 2010.

Takeshi Tada

Born in 1935. Graduated from Chuo University, Faculty of Law, passed the bar exam, 1957. Entered Legal Training and Research Institute of Japan, became Attorney at Law, registered with the Dai-ni Tokyo Bar Association, 1970. Established Tada Law Office, 1996. Has served as vice chairman of the Dai-ni Tokyo Bar Association; instructor in criminal defense at the Legal Training and Research Institute of Japan, chairman of the Legal Apprentice Training Committee, among others.

Shozaburo Ishida

Born in 1946. Graduated from Chuo University, Faculty of Law, passed the bar exam, 1969. Entered the Legal Training and Research Institute of Japan, 1971. Became an Attorney at Law registered with the Dai-ni Tokyo Bar Association, 1973. Established Sengoku & Ishida Law Office, 1983, reorganized as Ishida & Chinzei Law Office, 2007. Has served as chairman of the Criminal Defense Committee and deputy chairman of the Permanent Members Council of the Dai-ni Tokyo Bar

Association, and as vice chairman of the Criminal Defense Center of the Japan Federation of Bar Associations.

Masanori Ono

Born in 1948. Graduated from the University of Tokyo, Faculty of Law; passed the bar exam, 1972. Entered Legal Training and Research Institute of Japan, 1973. Became Attorney at Law, registered with the Dai-ni Tokyo Bar Association, 1975. Established Kamiyacho Law & Accounting Office, 1980; reorganized as New Tokyo Law & Accounting Office, 1980; reorganized as Tokyo Liberte, 2001. As an officer of the Dai-ni Tokyo Bar Association, has served as chairman of the Legal Apprentice Training Committee, Court Committee, and Criminal Defense Committee; as deputy chairman of the Permanent Members Council, vice chairman of the Dai-ni Tokyo Bar Association. As an officer of the Japan Federation of Bar Associations, has served as vice chairman of the Legal Apprentice Training Committee and Criminal Defense Center, deputy director of the Interrogation Visibility Realization Headquarters, acting director of the Lay Judge Headquarters, and Executive Governor, among other positions.

Etsuyoshi Izuta

Born in 1970. Passed the bar exam, 1993. Graduated from the University of Tokyo, Faculty of Law, entered the Legal Training and Research Institute of Japan,1994. Became Attorney at Law, registered with the Dai-ni Tokyo Bar Association, 1996. Shifted registry to the Shizuoka Bar Association, established Izuta Law Office, 2002. Established Libra Law Offices, 2005. Currently affiliated with the Hamamatsu Branch of the Shizuoka Bar Association; member of the Hakamada Case Subcommittee of the Human Rights Protection Committee of the Japan Federation of Bar Associations.

（英文版）取調べの「全面可視化」をめざして

STILL SEEKING JUSTICE

2011 年 3 月 29 日　第 1 刷発行

著　者	江副浩正、多田 武、石田省三郎、 小野正典、伊豆田悦義
発行者	廣田浩二
発行所	講談社インターナショナル株式会社 〒112-8652　東京都文京区音羽 1-17-14 電話　03-3944-6493（編集部）　　　　03-3944-6492（マーケティング部・業務部） ホームページ　www.kodansha-intl.com
印刷・製本所	大日本印刷株式会社

落丁本、乱丁本は購入書店名を明記のうえ、講談社インターナショナル業務部宛にお送りください。送料小社負担にてお取替えいたします。なお、この本についてのお問い合わせは、編集部宛にお願いいたします。定価はカバーに表示してあります。

Printed in Japan

ISBN 978-4-7700-3163-1